Remembering
PETER TOSH

Remembering
PETER

Compiled and edited by
Ceil Tulloch
Foreword by Garry Steckles

TOSH

IAN RANDLE PUBLISHERS
Kingston • Miami

First published in Jamaica, 2013 by
Ian Randle Publishers
11 Cunningham Avenue
Box 686
Kingston 6
www.ianrandlepublishers.com

Introduction and editorial material
© 2013 Ceil Tulloch

NATIONAL LIBRARY OF JAMAICA CATALOGUING-IN-
PUBLICATION DATA

Remembering Peter Tosh / compiled and edited by Ceil Tulloch

    p. : ill. ; cm.

ISBN 978-976-637-651-2 (pbk)

1. Tosh, Peter, 1944-1987   2. Reggae musicians – Jamaica
I. Tulloch, Ceil

782.42164092 - dc 23

Cover and Book Design by Ian Randle Publishers

Cover image : Sound check at the Roxy Theatre in Los
Angeles, California, 1983 © Roger Steffens/Roger Steffens's
Reggae Archives.

Printed and Bound in the China

In memoriam

For 'The Toughest'
(October 19, 1944 – September 11, 1987)

A luta continua

Contents

List of Illustrations

...the most rebellious, outspoken and politically conscious of the original Wailers...

Foreword
Memories of Peter Tosh
by Garry Steckles

I thought I had a few – until I read this book. I'll share just one of mine with you in a moment.

It's hard for me to compare with the treasure trove of anecdotes in the pages that follow about the man who will always be remembered as the most rebellious, outspoken and politically conscious of the original Wailers, attributes that often led to Peter being perceived negatively by people who didn't know him and/or didn't grasp what he was trying to do.

One of the things that struck me, the first time I was sent an advance manuscript by Ceil Tulloch, was that people who knew Peter much better than I did all regarded him the same way as me – just a great guy. Peter, despite whatever you may have read about him to the contrary, was kind, warm, generous, funny, outgoing and considerate. To be sure, he wasn't someone you wanted to annoy, but I did have the privilege of spending a fair amount of time with him in the days when I was promoting reggae concerts, and he was never – and I do mean never – difficult to get along with.

The chapters that follow are by no means the full story of Peter Tosh, but, until the definitive biography comes along, and I hope it does, they're a long-overdue testimony to a musician whose compelling story has been largely overshadowed by the global adulation that has been showered on his former Wailers band mate Bob Marley. It's not that Bob doesn't deserve all the accolades that have come his way, but Peter was much, much more than a footnote in the story of the Wailers and of reggae music in general, and deserves to be remembered as such.

The reminiscing of the all-star contributors Ceil roped in for this book triggered a rush of memories of my own. There's a reference, for example, to Peter playing at Ontario Place in Toronto, and recollections by Sly and Robbie of him leaving them alone on stage at the end of many concerts to showcase their own talents.

There was a bit of an overlap there in my personal memory bank. I was responsible for Peter's Ontario Place concert happening in the first place, got booed by an angry Jamaican crowd for my troubles, drove Peter to and from the gig and stood next to him, mesmerised, as he sang the final few minutes of his closing number backstage before we left the venue while Sly and Robbie kept the audience skanking.

The story started months before the actual gig, when Charles Comer, Peter's irrepressible publicist and one of my dearest friends, called from New York to tell me Peter would be touring and asking if I could help organise dates in Montreal, Ottawa and Toronto. Montreal was no problem. I took on that show myself, in partnership with André Menard and Alain Simard, the founders of the Montreal International Jazz Festival. We'd successfully promoted two previous Tosh shows in Montreal, and doing a third was a no-brainer. Ottawa was almost as easy. A local promoter who happened to be a big reggae fan snapped that one up for the evening after the Montreal show. Toronto, partly because of its massive Caribbean population, was the only problem. We had to find a place that could handle what we were sure would be a huge crowd, but the city's largest venues were simply too big and too expensive. So I decided to contact Ontario Place, the sprawling, government-owned entertainment complex on Toronto's waterfront, where the Forum, the facility's biggest concert showcase, routinely booked some of the biggest acts in the world, and, an important consideration, paid them extremely well.

At first, they were reluctant. Peter's rebel image and his tendency to smoke a little ganja on stage weren't exactly something they thought their Ontario government bosses would approve of. So off came the gloves. 'Aren't there tens of thousands – perhaps hundreds of thousands – of Caribbean people paying taxes in Ontario?' I asked. At the same time, I hinted gently that I might be using my journalistic connections (I'd worked at both the *Toronto Star* and *Globe* and *Mail* in the previous decade) to stir up some negative publicity, perhaps with racial connotations.

This got their full attention, and the date was soon added to Peter's calendar. The Montreal and Ottawa shows went off as planned, and we were on the road to Toronto, where there was enormous excitement in the city's Caribbean community about Peter playing at such a prestigious venue. And it didn't hurt that admission to Ontario Place concerts was free.

Peter's rebel image and his tendency to smoke a little ganja on stage weren't exactly something they thought their...bosses would approve of.

The Forum, where seating was first come, first served, was pretty much full hours before the show, as a mainly West Indian crowd arrived early to make sure they would have good seats. I was assigned – by Comer, who, as always, took total control of any show he was involved with – to drive Peter to and from Ontario Place, and we arrived to find the Forum jam-packed. Everything was going as planned until, ten minutes or so before show time, Forum officials started putting about four dozen seats on the stage. They were for VIPs (among them tennis great Bjorn Borg and the Jamaican ambassador to Canada), and there was an instant uproar. And, as anyone who's been to a few reggae shows can attest, a Jamaican crowd in a state of agitation is not something you would put on your wish list for an event.

The situation looked like it was getting out of hand, and Charles Comer, surveying the scene from the sidelines, was getting worried. This could mean negative publicity for Peter, and that, to the consummate PR man, was not something he could let happen. He grabbed me by the shoulder, propelled me towards the entrance to the amphitheatre, uttered words that still make me twitch. 'Get out there and see what you can do, Garry,' he said and then pushed me on to the stage.

The crowd, thinking I was the first VIP about to saunter out and choose my vantage point, immediately started howling abuse. This went on for a couple of minutes, but with a few musicians (perhaps taking pity on me) showing up on the stage the situation was quickly defused, although the irony of the crowd turning on the person who had been responsible for them seeing Peter Tosh for free has remained with me over the years.

The show was vintage Tosh, and the crowd – I'm delighted to say, not being one to hold a grudge – lapped it up.

After almost two hours, Peter started singing 'Babylon Queendom,' his usual closing number, and, with duty calling once more, I positioned myself beside our car ready to whisk him out of Ontario Place. The next thing I knew, he was walking straight towards me, still with the microphone in his hand and still singing. He was in another world, eyes closed, totally immersed in the music as he repeated the words 'Babylon, your queendom is falling, Rahab, Ethiopia calling,' time and again. This went on for two or three minutes, with Peter standing just inches from me, and I still get goosebumps thinking about it. Finally, he put down the microphone, and, with other band members leaving the stage one by one, we drove off, leaving Sly and Robbie keeping the crowd more than happy with straight-from-Yard drum and bass.

But enough from me – Sly and Robbie are waiting to tell you themselves about those concert finales, and many of Peter's other musical comrades in arms and good friends have stories to share that will add to your appreciation and understanding of a remarkable musician and an equally remarkable man.

One love,

Garry Steckles

Preface

*'I and I come with earthquake, lightning
and thunder to break down these barriers of
oppression, to drive away transgression and
rule equality between humble black people.'*
Peter Tosh
One Love Peace Concert
April 22, 1978

From 1963 to 1987, Peter Tosh battled against inequities
in his post-colonial homeland of Jamaica and also those in
South Africa, the Middle East and the USA. Constantly raging,
berating, fighting and exposing the hypocrisy and corruption
within the Establishment, and rallying the downtrodden to civil
disobedience, Tosh was peerless in his activism as an artist.
He tackled head-on the issues of apartheid, nuclear war,
police brutality, politics, poverty, and racism with a vengeance;
lashing conventional wisdom, offending the sensibilities
of those in power with his speech. When railing against the
political system, he coined the following words in his rhetoric:
'politricks,' 'crime ministers' and the 'House of Represent-a-
thief.' Armed with his caustic and sometimes witty, but always
relevant lyrics, Tosh waged his Jihad in the recording studio,
onstage and when interviewed.

Unrelenting in his mission to win the war against injustice,
this troubadour of the oppressed believed freedom was non-
negotiable. As far as he was concerned, there was no place
in the battle for ceasefires or political compromise. Eternally
taunting and repudiating the institution's veneer of justice and
equality, he made plain that the flawed system sorely needed
to be revamped. He made crystal clear his determination to

fix it. The system, or as he liked to call it, the 'shitstem,' must be subverted. A Moses to the disenfranchised, he was a 'Rod of Iron' to the guilty. Like a flea he would get under the skin of the old guard, raising their ire, provoking and challenging them to do the right thing, which was to dismantle the status quo. Believing wholeheartedly in his crusade, Tosh made no apologies for upsetting the applecart, even though he was at risk of losing his life.

A unique and creative force to be reckoned with, Tosh's mien and resonant voice always commanded the listener to pay full attention to his message and engage in soul-searching. Even when he began to climb up the rungs of the socio-economic ladder, Tosh remained an ally of the common man; he strongly identified with their plight, and spoke on their behalf. Unconcerned with being polished, his vernacular was plain yet fiery, and when he was sufficiently riled-up, very spicy. He did not mince words. When he spoke, Tosh left no doubt in the listener's mind of his stance on a particular topic. While some may take issue with his modus operandi, and/or dismiss his significant contributions to the realm of Reggae, none should however, refute the fact that he remained true to his convictions. Unflinching, he walked it like he talked it. He was the real McCoy.

On November 17, 2010, while enjoying videos on the internet of Peter Tosh's live performances, I began to ponder why his deeds of valour have not been adequately extolled. For a man of the people, whose legacy is primarily one of championing the rights of the underprivileged and bringing their plight and indignities suffered to the fore, it is a bit disconcerting that Tosh lived and died without much fanfare. Many years have elapsed since his death, yet few have stepped forward to advocate and ensure that he assume his rightful place in history. Perhaps

> *The system, or as he liked to call it, the 'shitstem,' must be subverted.*

this oversight or gross negligence on our part, as the case may be, is due to our limited understanding of him. Maybe, if we have a better grasp of his quintessence, posterity will be more charitable in its everlasting remembrance of him.

It is no secret that Tosh was fully cognisant of our apathy towards him and his craft, as evidenced by his 'livatribe' at the Jamaica World Music Festival, in Montego Bay, Jamaica on November 27, 1982. There, he declared, 'Many of you underestimated the qualities and potential of my music and also underestimated my ability…but I'm not here to exalt myself. I am here to exalt the name of JAH….' While he certainly did not need or expect our validation, should that exonerate us from paying him due homage for his resolve to make the world an equitable place? Although discussions about culpability are never sexy, and it is not the purpose of this book to engage in discourse about moral obligation, I sincerely hope that in the near future, more historians will examine the breadth and depth of this reggae warrior's impact on music and beyond.

Tosh's intention to heighten our knowledge about himself and his deep-rooted ethical conviction is apparent by the Red X cassettes he had been recording in anticipation of writing his autobiography. Unfortunately, he was deprived of the opportunity to pen his memoir. While it is commendable that several authors have found it fitting to write about Tosh, and there have been a smattering of symposiums and roundtables devoted to honouring him, over a quarter of a century later, he is still relegated to a mere footnote in the annals of Jamaican music. Hence, this collection of short stories provides remembrances of Tosh's life that are comprehensive in scope.

Although Tosh would be martyred at the age of 42 and remembered primarily for the militant nature of his songs, I believe that his forcefulness was just one aspect of his multifaceted personality. Completely enthralled by this controversial, musical giant's work and interested in learning more about his life away from the public limelight, in the spring of 2011, I decided to contact as many of his associates as possible, and ask them to share their recollections of him that would shed light on his character, wit, generosity of spirit, etc. After all, their collective reminiscences would be beneficial in drawing us a more fully-delineated portrait of their comrade. As such, in mid-May, I commenced my mission. I was both delighted and touched by the alacrity (some replied within half of an hour of receiving my email, others within a day or two), and the enthusiasm of those who responded. 'Sign me up!' 'Count me in!' 'Anything for Peter Tosh.' These are a few of the many wonderful messages I received in response to my solicitation. Additionally, several of these individuals also thoughtfully referred me to other colleagues and friends of Mr Tosh for inclusion in this project.

Over the course of my conversations with all the contributors, I was privy to information that enabled me to gain further insight into the inner core of Peter Tosh. You have in your possession a patchwork of memories about a special man, his mission and music. You hold in your hands a compilation of tributes by those who were privileged to know him personally and/or professionally. It is my hope that their concerted recollections will not only enable us to unravel the enigma that shrouds Mr Tosh, but will eventually lead to his proper and accurate alignment in history.

Acknowledgements

This book would not have materialised without the support of the following illustrious individuals:

Garry Steckles, whose music and culture column for *Caribbean Beat* is always a delight to read, is uniquely qualified to write the foreword to this book. He was personally acquainted with Mr Tosh and is himself a highly respected author and journalist with more than four decades of experience working for major newspapers in the UK, Canada, the USA and Caribbean. Furthermore, I am also indebted to him for his spirited support and noble efforts to publicise this tribute to a genuine master of reggae music. *Respect.*

In Jamaica

Herbie Miller, who gave courage and steadfast faith in the project at moments of doubt, was extraordinarily generous with his time, resources and memories. He also opened the door of communication to several other participants and assisted with marketing the book. I am also grateful to him for his gesture of confidence in my ability to tell Mr Tosh's story. I hope that I have done it justice.

Dermot Hussey was a great source of support and wisdom. His immense help with contacts in the entertainment community, kindness in sharing his personal recollections of Mr Tosh with me and assistance with marketing the book were deeply appreciated.

Desmond 'Shakes' Shakespeare's exuberance rallied my spirits during difficult times, while his treasure trove of memories enabled me to understand Mr Tosh on many levels. I would also like to take this opportunity to thank Shakes for his assistance in getting the book published.

Dr Omar Davies, MP, gets my heartfelt appreciation for taking time out of his busy day to provide social commentary that contextualises Mr Tosh's place in Jamaica's history.

Lowell 'Sly' Dunbar and **Robbie Shakespeare** get my deepest gratitude for their wonderful and vivid accounts of jamming with Mr Tosh that greatly contributed to my understanding of this very complex man.

Hosannas for the **Reverend Canon Ernle P. Gordon,** retired rector of the Church of St Mary the Virgin, whose contribution provides an interesting perspective of Mr Tosh's music in regard to theology.

Rupert Lewis, PhD, Associate Director of the Centre of Caribbean Thought at the University of the West Indies at Mona, must be singled out and thanked for his boundless support in reviewing my manuscript and providing a blurb.

I am grateful to **Leslie Franklin** of Sunset Tiverton Inn, Bluefields, Westmoreland, for his invaluable assistance in expediting and securing input from one of Mr Tosh's most ardent supporters.

In Canada

Norman 'Otis' Richmond, whose encyclopedic knowledge of all aspects of black history and culture is astounding, gets a special mention for kindly providing us with a more nuanced portrait of Mr Tosh. *Asante Sana.*

Colin Lee, who was a perceptive reader of my manuscript, gets a special 'big up' for volunteering to read my drafts and providing useful suggestions. Additionally, his wise counsel throughout the project kept me sane. *A jus luv still.*

In England

Colin Grant, independent historian, Associate Fellow in the Centre for Caribbean Studies, author, and producer at BBC radio, receives encomium for his invaluable assessment of my work. My gratitude also overflows to Sonia Grant, Colin Grant's uber-efficient freelance publicist, who was an extremely gracious and helpful liaison.

In Germany

Wolfgang Gürster, of rock-shot.com, is an absolute gem for generously proffering courtesy images from his rock collection and for the steadfast encouragement along the way. *Danke*

In South Korea

James Klipper receives two thumbs up for editing my Introduction and giving me a refresher course on the proper placement of that all-important comma. *You rock!*

A very warm thanks goes to **Jung-Tae Kim, PhD,** for providing crucial technical support.

In Trinidad

Jeremy Taylor, Managing Director, MEP, merits particular thanks for his kind referral.

In the USA

Roger Steffens, whose inexhaustible knowledge of reggae music and culture was indispensable for my research, deserves rounds of applause for his unfailing generosity of spirit. Not only did he graciously extend himself to honour my several *huge* requests for assistance, but thoughtfully provided trenchant anecdotes of Mr Tosh, valuable comments on my writing, and in a gesture of magnanimity put at my disposal his prized photographs of Tosh, many little known and unpublished. Ras Rojah, nuff thanks!

Chuck Krall, who during the course of this project has become a friend, is to be lauded for his unwavering support, entertaining snapshot recollections of Mr Tosh during the 1970s and incredible images which made the book extra special.

Dick Wingate receives my copious thanks for adding in-depth knowledge about the efforts that were expended in marketing and promoting *Legalise It,* and for sharing illuminating stories about Mr Tosh's relationship with the music industry. Moreover, he was a veritable support system for marketing the book.

I am incalculably indebted to the late **Jayne Cortez, George 'Fully' Fullwood, Donald Kinsey and Dennis Thompson** for their wonderful revelations about their and Mr Tosh's artistic and personal friendships which provided penetrating insights into his personality and were invaluable to this work. Dennis also gets additional kudos for his generous donation of one of his images.

I have benefitted as well from **Frances Fullwood's** warmth and pertinent responses, which made the process much less stressful.

Doug Wendt also deserves huge accolades. His fascinating reminiscences were deeply appreciated.

I would also like to especially thank **Kate Fagan Burgun** of Heavy Manners and **Abayomi Azikiwe** of Pan-African News Wire File Photos, for generously allowing me to use Jim Pasta's photo of Messrs Tosh, Thompson and Kinsey and Eliza Richmond's image of Messrs Richmond and Tosh respectively.

Avrom Robin, Susan Finkelstein, Kim Gottlieb-Walker, Jim Pasta and **Matte Hucke** deserve a million 'thank yous' for their magnanimous contribution of visually arresting images which enliven this compilation.

E.M. Heinlein, whose meticulous eye and insight never ceases to inspire has my eternal gratitude for all her encouragement along the way. Her crucial role in offering sound advice, concrete help, and instructions on writing effectively will always be cherished. Edith, you are a true friend, wonderful cicerone and a real trooper!

Roderick Thomson, who is a constant source of inspiration and wisdom, has my unfailing love and appreciation.

Alethia Lee gets big hugs for cheerfully and generously assisting with this, that, and the other. *Mi luv yu fi dat!*

I am indebted to **Anthony DaCosta** for sharing online footage of Mr Tosh's Thanksgiving service which was a vital resource in my narrative.

Ian Randle, publisher at Ian Randle Publishers Ltd, and his superb team, all get my heartfelt thanks for seeing the merit in this project and for making this book a reality.

And finally, I salute *Worrell King*, CEO of King of Kings Promotions, who deserves praise for steadfastly keeping Mr Tosh's memory alive in Jamaica through his annual Peter Tosh Tribute Show and Symposium.

Ceil Tulloch
Daejeon, S. Korea
June 2012

...Tosh had lived his life as a devout Rasta...

Introduction:
A Biographical Sketch of Peter Tosh

September 27, 1987

The National Arena in Kingston, Jamaica was partially filled with people on this warm and sunny Sunday. The assembled, however, were not gathered for a business, political, or entertainment event. They were there to attend a function of far greater magnitude – the Thanksgiving service for the reggae rebel, Peter Tosh. Family, friends, associates and the common man who admired Tosh, occupied the facility. Others queued along the streets in the immediate vicinity to pay their respects. While Tosh had lived his life as a devout Rasta, he was given a complimentary Christian funeral by the very same Jamaican government with which he had a contentious and sometimes volatile relationship. Despite the Establishment's decision to bestow this honour on the 'Steppin' Razor,' with the exception of law enforcement officers, other representatives of the order were conspicuously absent.

Concessions however were made to accommodate Tosh's Rastafari and Pan-African beliefs. The dais on which his casket laid was swathed in the tri-colours of the Ethiopian flag and likewise Rasta colours of red, green and gold. A large image of Jamaica's first national hero Marcus Mosiah Garvey, who Tosh respected as a prophet, was prominently displayed in the foreground of an illustration of the African continent. Images of HIM Haile Selassie also held a position of prominence in the background.

Throughout the funeral service, there were readings from the Scriptures, prayers offered, singing, and music (including Tosh's own beautiful composition 'Creation'). Acclaimed

Jamaican saxophonist Dean Fraser performed a stirring rendition of Jimmy Cliff's ballad 'Many Rivers to Cross.' Four members of the Ethiopian Orthodox Tewahedo Church's clergy officiated the service. At predetermined intervals throughout Tosh's service, the four priests circled and blessed the casket. The solemn procession is led by the cleric carrying a cross, while the arch deacon, who at precise moments swings the censure, brings up the rear. Celebrated musicologist, media personality, and author, Dermot Hussey, delivered the eulogy.

Similar to his life, Tosh's death was not devoid of drama. As such, his service was punctuated by tragicomical incidents. In watching footage of Tosh's funeral service, the viewer sees a young man armed with a large banner with the word FREEDOM written in large, capital, red letters, bordered in the three colours of the United Negro Improvement Association (UNIA) flag (red, black and green) which is symbolic of African nationhood and was devised by Garvey. During the service, he thought it opportune for him to make his political statement to the public. As such, he interrupted the proceedings by parading for several minutes in front of the congregants, defying the authorities when they attempted to stop his mission. He was eventually escorted outside of the building.

Similar to his life, Tosh's death was not devoid of drama.

The climax, however, was reached when an older man carrying a staff, clad in a white cap, shirt and trousers, mounted the platform. Standing directly in front of the closed casket, he commanded Peter to 'arise and open the casket.' After several tense minutes, when it became apparent that Peter was not about to follow in Lazarus's footsteps, the man then beseeched the absent Prime Minister to 'open the casket.' When that wish also went unheeded, he enquired, 'Mr Prime Minister, why did you kill Peter?'

While his transgression may have provided humour for some people, who were inclined to think 'him head nuh good,' thoughts on the involvement of foul play in Tosh's death did not seem so far-fetched to others. After all, there had been rumblings in certain pockets of society, initially behind closed doors, about the real circumstances surrounding Tosh's demise. It was not merely the fact that Tosh and two of his friends were killed in a robbery attempt that appeared to have gotten terribly out of control, which people found unpalatable, but the additional knowledge that the victims were shot execution style left a distinct aftertaste. Moreover, despite all the bloodshed, very little property was removed from Tosh's premises. Basil Walters, a *Jamaica Observer* Staff Reporter in his article, 'Lest We Forget Peter Tosh, Free I, Doc Brown,' published on Sunday, September 13, 2009, reported that all the decedents had been shot once or twice in their heads while the survivors suffered multiple bullet wounds to various parts of their bodies.

When news reports broadcasted the latest developments in the case, private thoughts were voiced publicly by some in certain circles, and speculation became rife that more sinister motives were indeed at work. For some people, Tosh's aura of intrepidity made his death the more shocking and cast a pall of gloom over the music society.

The horrific tragedy occurred early in the night of September 11, 1987, at Tosh's Barbican residence in Kingston, shortly after he had returned from a business trip to the USA. While relaxing with his common law wife, Andrea Marlene Brown, and three other guests – his drummer Carlton Davis, the herbalist Wilton 'Doc' Brown and musician Michael Robinson – three intruders, one of whom was later identified as Dennis Lobban, barged into Tosh's home. During the bedlam, popular JBC radio disc jockey, Jeff 'Free I' Dixon and his wife, Yvonne who had been invited over earlier and were expected, arrived. After the assassins made several demands of Tosh for money, to which he replied that he had none on hand, they opened fire on him and his associates. Tosh, Brown, and 'Free I' Dixon would eventually succumb to their wounds. At the time of his passing, Tosh was five weeks shy of celebrating his forty-third birthday.

While death by murder is always tragic, media reports on Tosh's passing away shocked fans around the globe because of the sheer senselessness of the act. The public understood that this atrocity did more than just rob the world of an edutainer. It was evident to those who knew and/or understood what Tosh was about that the effect of this crime transcended the parameters of the music fraternity. They were keenly aware that this offence not only permanently silenced the powerful voice of a music icon, but also that of a staunch advocate for Black liberation and disenfranchised people worldwide.

Tosh, who was christened Winston Hubert McIntosh, hailed from the rural, agricultural town of Grange Hill, which is located in the scenic, fishing parish of Westmoreland. From a very early age, he showed signs of being a wunderkind. In an August 19, 1983, radio interview that Tosh did with Mel Cheplowitz on UC Berkeley KALX 90.7 FM, he disclosed that,

> He started singing at age two, played an instrument at three, made his own instrument from a piece of board and a sardine can with a couple of strings attached to it at age five – which people paid him to play for them. And at age seven, he began performing on stage songs and poems that he had learnt at school.

Furthermore, Tosh informed Cheplowitz that 'at age 13, he had six months practical piano forte music lessons and had reached fifth grade when he was forced to stop taking lessons.'

At approximately age 15, Tosh relocated to Kingston, Jamaica's capital and largest city. He lived in Denham Town prior to settling in the community of Trench Town, which is known for the vast number of talented musicians it has produced over the decades in the music genres of ska, rocksteady and reggae. During the early 1960s, Tosh had the good fortune to meet his future band mates and close friends – Neville 'Bunny Wailer' Livingston and Robert 'Bob' Marley. The triad quickly established a rapport with each other and became the core members of the group, The Wailers which they formed with three other pals – Junior Braithwaite, Cherry Green, and later, Beverley Kelso. Similar to other youths in the community who were pursuing their musical aspirations, the group would benefit from the mentorship of Joe Higgs, a respected musician.

Keeping abreast of the popular music of the era, The Wailers played ska at music venues in Kingston. They would in the course of time, come to the attention of record producer, Clement 'Sir Coxson' Dodd. The affable and incomparable American reggae archivist/ actor/media personality/author/ lecturer/photojournalist Roger Steffens, who has played an integral role in promoting the global awareness of reggae music on multiple levels since 1973, and who wholeheartedly

'reggae is the chosen rhythm of resistance around the world,...'

believes that 'reggae is the chosen rhythm of resistance around the world,' explains how the group ended up recording on the Coxsone label.

Higgs, who was having major battles with Coxson over nonpayment of royalties was opposed to The Wailers auditioning for Dodd. Alvin 'Seeco' Patterson, – who had befriended the youths and would later become the percussionist in Bob Marley's newly formed Wailers band after his split from Tosh and Livingston – encouraged them to audition and set up the test, much against Joe's wishes. Neither Joe nor Seeco accompanied the group to their audition. Unimpressed with their performance, Dodd sent them away. Upon their return, Seeco asked them if they had sung 'Simmer Down.' When they replied, 'No,' he sent them back immediately to have Coxson hear that song. Bunny told me that Coxson was so impressed that they returned to Dodd's Studio One the next morning to record it. Incidentally, in a conversation I had previously with

Dodd, he clarified the different spellings of his name. When referring to him, the man, his name is spelt Coxson In regard to his label or the sound system, it is Coxsone.

The song 'Simmer Down,' which was a huge commercial success across Jamaica in 1964, helped to establish the group's popularity with Jamaican audiences. Furthermore, Tosh also recorded the single 'I'm the Toughest' and the humourous 'Shame and Scandal' on Dodd's label.

Due to personal reasons, several of the original members of the group eventually left. So, the team would ultimately consist of Tosh, Livingston and Marley. Together, they produced several more hits for Studio One, before making the decision to part company with Dodd after their relationship became strained over issues pertaining to compensation.

Tosh also recorded several songs and instrumentals under the pseudonym Peter Touch

When the opportunity arose for Marley to temporarily live and work in Delaware, Tosh and Livingston kept the group afloat by recruiting Rita Marley's cousin and fellow member of the Soulettes, Constantine 'Dream'/'Vision' Walker, Jr to stand in for Bob.

An occurrence in April 1966, which would have monumental impact on the triumvirate's personal and professional lives, was the arrival in Jamaica of HIM Haile Selassie I, a.k.a. Ras Tafari Makonnen. Regarded by Rastafari as the black Messiah, the late emperor's physical presence on the island corroborated, for the trio, information that they had read in the Bible. Confirmation of this biblical prophecy led the friends to adapt the Rastafarian philosophy and spiritual lifestyle. This shift also became apparent in their music which now took on a more spiritual tone. Tosh specifically, in addition to making the decision to become a devout Rasta, duly inspired by Selassie's visit to his homeland, penned the song 'Rasta Shook Them Up.'

By the time Marley returned to Jamaica and reunited with his band mates, rocksteady was all the rage. As such, the triad altered their music style and prepared to segue into the new genre. Seeking autonomy and complete control over their output, the friends decided to form their own independent record label, Wail'n Soul/Wail 'N' Soul'M. For recordings on their new label, the group went by the name of Bob Marley and the Wailing Wailers.

After a short and challenging stint of running their own record label the trio formed a brief alliance with the influential Chinese-Jamaican producer Leslie Kong. During their collaboration, they recorded the album, *The Best of the Wailers,* on Kong's Beverly's label; it was released the summer of 1971 shortly before Kong's untimely death from a heart attack in early August. On this album, listeners are treated to Tosh singing lead vocals on songs such as 'Stop the Train,' 'Can't You See' and 'Soon Come.'

Steffens recalls that during the end of the 1960s and early 1970s, Tosh also recorded several songs and instrumentals under the pseudonym Peter Touch for several producers including Joe Gibbs and Tony Robinson. On Jackpot Records, produced by Bunnie Lee (1969), he recorded the upbeat 'Moon Duck' as well as 'The Crimson Pirate'. While on the Unity label for Randy's, he recorded 'The Return of Al Capone.' For Prince Buster's Olive Blossom imprint Tosh recorded 'Simpleton' and numerous other instrumentals. 'Many were recorded without his knowledge, and found only on UK labels.'

An association was also formed with the musical maverick, reggae producer Lee 'Scratch' Perry during this period. This partnership was mutually beneficial for all parties concerned and The Wailers once again enjoyed local success on the air waves and in clubs. During this era, Tosh also began to demonstrate his pensive nature and released conscious songs such as 'Four Hundred Years,' 'No Sympathy,' and 'Downpressor' on Perry's Upsetter label. Additionally, he released empowering songs such as 'Arise Blackman' and 'Black Dignity' plus, the cautionary 'Can't Blame the Youth' as singles.

The advent of the 1970s brought another pivotal change in the lives of all three Wailers. After craving international success for quite some time, they finally got their big break in 1972 when they signed a contract with the tony English record label Island Records. After the moderate success of their first two albums for Island (*Catch A Fire* and *Burnin'*), but dissatisfied with the status quo, Tosh and Livingston decided to quit the band and embark on their own solo careers.

From the mid-1970s, Tosh formed his own band, Word, Sound and Power, his record label Intel Diplo HIM, and produced many songs of a socio-political nature. Furthermore, he also recorded with several major record labels including Virgin, Columbia, and later on, EMI. While these recordings found favour with a healthy segment of the population, they were not as popular with the mainstream audience. The appeal of Tosh's music would however increase after he entered into contract with the English rock band the Rolling Stones. While their collaboration took some of Tosh's fans by surprise, his ability to win over rock patrons allowed him to garner a fairly impressive share of the international market – especially in the USA and Canada.

Esteemed English music journalist and author Garry Steckles, who had the pleasure of promoting and arranging several of Tosh's tours in Montreal and Toronto, provides greater insight into Tosh's prominence in the late seventies and early eighties, a time in which he was touring virtually non-stop, mainly in North America and Europe.

Says Steckles:

> Peter made a very, very clever move that had nothing to do with making music or performing on stage. He brought on board a first-class publicist. Reggae musicians, by and large, have rarely paid much attention to the marketing and promotion side of the business, but Bob and Peter were both smart enough to realise they could create the most wonderful

music, but that without professional help in bringing it to the attention of potential listeners outside of the Caribbean, they simply weren't going to attract the sort of audience they deserved. It's no coincidence – at least in my book – that the two most commercially successful, as well as critically acclaimed, artists in the history of Jamaican music knew how important it was to have a sophisticated PR operation.

I was involved in promoting several Tosh concerts in Montreal during this era, and was impressed by how willing Peter was to be interviewed, to cooperate when it came to promoting concerts, and how generally media savvy he was. We never had any problems selling out his shows in Montreal, but Peter was always willing to help ensure the concerts attracted maximum media coverage, as well as filling the venue.

One of my vivid memories of Peter was in Toronto when he was about to appear at Ontario Place in 1980. Peter's hotshot publicist, Charles Comer, had arranged an interview with CBC television, but it *...the mid-1970s, Tosh formed his own band, Word, Sound and Power...* was at the outrageously early hour – for a reggae musician – of 9:30 a.m. I was on the road with Peter and the band, and was delegated by Charles to pick up he and Peter at their hotel and drive them to the CBC studios. We knocked on Peter's door around 8:30 a.m. and a sleepy looking Tosh, in his underwear and with a big spliff in his hand, looked decidedly weary when we walked into his room. Charles took command of the situation instantly: 'Peter Tosh, get yourself dressed and put that spliff out this minute. You can't be late for the CBC.' I waited, somewhat apprehensively, for Peter to kick us both out of the room amid a barrage of succinct and unprintable Jamaican cussing. Instead, he took a semi-defiant final toke on the spliff and said, quietly, 'Okay, Charlie, I'll be right with you.' He got dressed immediately, and we were comfortably on time for the interview.

I think my other lingering memory of Peter is that despite his reputation for having something of a short fuse, he was perfectly easy to get along with as long as the people he was dealing with didn't go out of their way to provoke him. I had to pick him up at Montreal's Dorval airport on one occasion, when he was on the Wanted Dread and Alive tour, and an official wasn't happy with Peter's documents, so I was called into the immigration area to sort things out. Peter had simply decided not to get involved, and stood quietly to one side while I explained to the official that all his papers were in order, showed him a work permit and gave him a poster to the show. A situation that could have become a problem was defused quickly and amicably, and that was all down to Peter.

In the USA, Tosh was a most welcomed performer at music venues, particularly on the West and East Coasts. Additionally, he was the guest artist on popular shows such as Saturday Night Live and the David Letterman Show, and a favourite interviewee for numerous media personalities. Despite his burgeoning popularity and legions of fans across North America and Europe, according to Tosh's comments in interviews, the large record labels were reticent to market his music in the manner he desired. Frustrated, Tosh, after the release of his 1983 album, *Mama Africa,* went into self-imposed exile in Africa for several years starting in 1984.

...Peter would have been appalled at the circumstances of a state funeral...

Steffens, who had the privilege of several tête-à-têtes with Tosh, recalls that on one occasion when he interviewed him, they discussed his plan to settle in Africa. Tosh informed Steffens that his future would be in Africa because he was tired of being abused by the system. He wrote the song 'Mama Africa' to tell her (Africa) that he was coming home, and that his move to Africa should not be interpreted to mean that he was going into exile.

Reflecting on Tosh's relationship with Africa, Steffens mentions the following:

> His militance about overcoming the yoke of colonialism made him a hero to liberation movements and militants of every description in Africa. As for Tosh in Africa, I only know from Olatunji and others that his trip to Nigeria did not go well. I think his experiences there and in Swaziland opened his eyes to the reality of Africa, and I never heard him express a specific part of the continent to which he would like to return.

Upon Tosh's return to Jamaica and the studio, he recorded and released his final studio album, *No Nuclear War,* on the EMI label shortly before he was assassinated. In 1988, he was posthumously awarded a Grammy for 'Best Reggae Album.'

While some may opine that Tosh's early rendezvous with death was inevitable when his radicalism is taken into consideration, such musings were not the concern of those assembled to bid him adieu at the National Arena on September 27, 1987. United in their grief, the attendees wanted to show their appreciation for a man who they felt was a great humanitarian and also a credit to both Jamaica and the music industry.

Hussey in his moving funeral oration, attested to the fact that Tosh's '…fame never shook the things he believed in: Rastafari, black nationalism and the legalisation of ganja.' Mulling over Tosh and his funeral service Hussey remarks,

> I think Peter would have been appalled at the circumstances of a state funeral, but those are the ironies that we often have to contend with. One of the sad things about Peter's funeral was how sparsely it was attended. The mood in the country at the time of his death and the low funeral turnout, remain an embarrassment. I did not see, or feel a sense of great loss, or any outpouring of grief, except by those very close to him. One thing still remains in my mind, and that was the remark of a white foreigner, who attended the funeral. His accent seemed as if he could have been either Irish or Scottish. He said, 'Jamaica, you are a terrible country because

you kill some of your best people,' or words to that effect. His vox pop was recorded by JBC/TV.

The mystery surrounding why he was slain and some of the names associated with this heinous crime remain unsolved. However, many of his admirers take solace in the fact that justice was partially served when the jury returned with a verdict of guilty during Dennis Lobban's murder trial. Lobban, a former street vendor, and acquaintance of Tosh from their youth, and who had been the beneficiary of Tosh's largesse on several occasions, was positively identified by two of the survivors of the shooting as being one of the assailants.

According to a document filed by Lobban with the Human Rights Committee on January 16, 1998 that is on file at the University of Minnesota Human Rights Library collection, entitled, *Dennis Lobban v Jamaica*, on June 17, 1988, the author was convicted of three counts of murder in the Home Circuit Court of Kingston and sentenced to death. His appeal against conviction was rejected by the Court of Appeal on June 4, 1990. On November 30, 1992, he applied for special leave to appeal to the Judicial Committee of the Privy Council. On February 10, 1993, he was granted leave to appeal. On April 6, 1995, his appeal was dismissed. On July 21, 1995, the author's death sentence was commuted to life imprisonment. It is submitted that the author is unable to pursue a constitutional motion, because of his financial situation and the unavailability of legal aid for the purpose.

12

Through the Lens

A Portfolio of Pictures

of Peter Tosh

In Jamaica, mid-1970s
© Avrom Robin/Susan Finkelstein

E WORLD MESSAGES

R THE POOR SHALL

VER CEASE OUT OF THE

ND.... DEUT. 15:11.

HOU SHALT NOT KILL.

EXODUS, 20:13.

WILL MAKE THY SEED

THE DUST... GEN. 13:1

E WAY SIDE GOSPEL.

...a warrior spirit, a man who was very sensitised to injustice.

Sound check at the Roxy Theatre in Los Angeles, California, 1983 for his last show in LA
©Roger Steffens/Roger Steffens's Reggae Archives

Musings on
a Warrior Spirit
by Dermot Hussey

I see Peter as a warrior spirit, a man who was very sensitised to injustice. He was deeply aware of slavery and our colonial past and, indeed, that we had been largely unable to put that past behind us. I admired the fact that Peter used his musical talent to amplify those issues. On one occasion, I even participated with him in a march against Ian Smith's Rhodesia.

My impressions of Peter are not long term, but largely of the period when he was managed by my friend, Herbie Miller, and I accompanied him, Peter and his band, Word, Sound and Power, to Brazil. Previously, I was very aware of him as a Wailer, and had seen him perform and watched the group's rehearsals. However, it was not until I accompanied Peter to a festival in São Paulo, and spent nine days in Rio de Janeiro with him, that our relationship really developed. That experience resulted in me writing a feature for the *Jamaica Daily Gleaner* newspaper, and subsequently, doing both a radio and some TV features on him as well.

As our relationship blossomed, I came to appreciate Peter's humour and warmth. He was funny in the way he turned words around, giving them new meaning, and highlighting some of the ironies of life both in Jamaica and the world at large. I also found amusing the way he told stories about his experiences – some of them quite mystical – regarding his desire to fly, and things of that nature.

One of my favourite recollections of Peter's wit is an incident that occurred at the Miami International Airport on our return from Brazil. Prior to our departure from Jamaica, a waiver had to be sought from the American Embassy in Kingston to allow

Peter to be in transit in Miami, since he had previously been denied a visa because of a ganja charge. On approaching US Customs, we encountered an officer who seemed confident that he might find ganja on Peter's person. In a beautifully timed moment of pre-emption, Peter stuck his hands into his jacket pocket and said, 'I have no ganja today, but here is a seed.' The official, completely disarmed by Peter's humour, laughed. Peter also had a generosity of spirit, and in physical terms was very generous in helping others.

In terms of the strained relationship he had with the Jamaican authority, I believe that the roots of his defiance sprang from several sources, namely, his being politically conscious, and a refusal to accept without challenge, our colonial past, the political, cultural, and social conditions of Africa, and being a black man in this world. All these factors led to Peter being misunderstood, largely by his own people, especially as his stance was uncompromising, and few of us are prepared to, 'Get Up, Stand Up.'

Due to life experiences disrupting his trajectory, Peter's enormous talent remained largely unfulfilled. I hope that over time, Jamaicans and a wider audience beyond our shores will regard him as an unsung warrior.

Reflections on
a Straight Shooter

by Norman O. Richmond

Peter was a very friendly, intelligent and articulate man. He was quite outspoken, but also a very kind person. I think people came to him with a lot of foolishness which caused him to express himself negatively, but in general, I found him to be a very gentle person.

I first met Peter in 1978 or 1979, in Los Angeles when he was in town to do some shows. At the time, I was based in Toronto and had previously written articles about Peter for a black weekly newspaper in Toronto called *Contrast*. My employer sent me to Los Angeles to interview Peter prior to his performance at a club which was scheduled for the following night. Since my mother is a reggae aficionado, I invited her to accompany me on the assignment.

When we arrived at our destination, Peter was inside watching the Wide World of Sports television series and cursing up a storm. As soon as Peter saw my mother, he toned down his language. I remember that he was very polite to my mother and even invited her to come down to Jamaica. His behaviour informed me that he had a lot of respect for elders.

At the end of my first interview with Peter, I was left with the impression that he was very articulate, funny – his sense of humour was very evident – and overall, very serious about the plight of black people. I think that his having a good command of the English language is probably the reason why Bob Marley made him the spokesperson of the band. While Bob was also capable of expressing himself in English, I think that he preferred to have Peter do the talking.

In subsequent interviews, as I got to know Peter better, I came to admire his militancy and directness. I think that his militancy, however, really hurt him in the music industry because he was a little bit too outspoken and his honesty cost him fans. I used to tell people that Peter could not have been a Calypsonian because the double entendre was not his thing; he was a straight shooter. Unlike Calypso artists, such as the Mighty Sparrow, who would put people down in their music while giving the unsuspecting listener the impression that they were being praised, Peter was always forthright. He was like the late Patrice Lumumba of the Congo, who always stood up and did not accept any BS.

From my conversations with Peter, the thing that impressed me the most about him was his commitment to the struggle of African people. On one occasion when I was interviewing him on my radio show, he explained to me that he had been inspired to write the lyrics for his song 'Apartheid,' after he had watched the news on TV and witnessed the white South Africans shooting their black compatriots. I found the way that he articulated that sentiment to be very powerful.

During his heyday, Peter was a popular performer in Toronto and had played here about five or six times. He used to perform at a huge venue called Ontario Place, which had a seating capacity of around 10,000 patrons. He was also well-known to the media because he gave great interviews.

...his militancy, however, really hurt him in the music industry because he was a little bit too outspoken and his honesty cost him fans.

On one occasion when Peter toured Canada, his manager, Herbie Miller, who I was already acquainted with through some Jamaican friends we had in common, invited me to join them. So, I did and basically just jumped on the bus with them. While touring with them, Peter and I would argue a lot about secular and religious matters because he knew that I was a secularist. We would talk a lot about socialism and capitalism. I used to tell him that I was a socialist, and he would always have a fit. Then I would ask him about the kind of economic system he believed in and declare that it could only be capitalism, or socialism, which would eventually lead to communism. He would go off when I made those comments and proceed to talk about all the isms and schisms.

The last time that Peter was in Toronto – I believe it was in 1985 or 1986 – he and I spent the whole day together. His publicist, the late Charlie Comer, and I rode with him in a limousine to several sporting goods stores and bookstores. One of them was called Third World Bookstore, and was owned by a first generation Canadian couple named Lynn and Gwen Johnson, who were of Jamaican and American heritage respectively. We also visited a surplus store called Honest Ed, where Peter bought some goggles and other equipment. I vividly recall that while we rode in the limousine the love song, 'How Bout Us,' by Champaign, was playing on the radio and

Richmond and Tosh, Los Angeles 1978/1979

by Eliza Richmond
©*Abayomi Azikiwe of Pan African News Wire File Photos*

Peter sang the whole song – word for word. Since I was familiar with the history of The Wailers music, I teased him and said, 'I thought that you did not like those kinds of lyrics?' He just burst out laughing and asked, 'What kind of music do you think that I make love to my woman to?' While Peter did not really record or perform love songs, he was not opposed to them.

Throughout the day, we also spent time talking about his love of flying kites and discussing, at length, the subject of Africa because he knew that I was very knowledgeable about that topic. Many people are under the impression that Americans are clueless about Africa. I would get a kick out of their views because I knew that I could hold my own with anybody on that subject. Peter was duly impressed that I could keep up with him on matters related to Africa and we would engage in serious discourse. I believe that we hit it off immediately because of our common interest in Africa. Throughout the course of our discussions, Peter would comment that it did not matter where a black person was born, she or he was still an African. That statement of his has stayed with me over the years.

The last time I spoke with Peter, I was interviewing him and he was visibly upset about his dealings with the record labels. He was in general, having problems with the music industry.

When I heard the news about Peter's death, I was at home with my wife and listening to the radio. I was very shocked by the announcement and pretty torn up about it. I said to myself, 'Here we go again! Malcolm X, Patrice Lumumba, Fred Hampton, Alprentice 'Bunchy' Carter....' I just reflected on the litany of black people who had been assassinated by the state – whether they were police, or assassins hired to do the job. Peter was actually the second person that I personally knew who died under those unfortunate circumstances. When he died, I was getting ready to go and visit him, as the UN was scheduled to have a conference on apartheid which I planned to attend.

In retrospect, I wish that I could have had the opportunity to visit Peter on his turf and check out his music collection.

In terms of music, Peter was very fond of European classical music and enjoyed listening to Tchaikovsky. I remember that his associates liked to make fun of his taste in music. On one occasion, while on tour with Peter and his band, when we got off the bus, his Jamaican guitarist Mikey Chung said, 'Charlie Parker, Sly, and Robbie listen to George Clinton, while Peter listens to Tchaikovsky. Nobody is listening to reggae.' I believe that Peter's interest in classical music also played a role in making his own music very sophisticated. He was not just a 'One Drop' man, he had range.

While Peter had eclectic taste in music, he was not crazy about jazz and used to criticise that genre of music by saying, 'It sounds like bees in a hive,' which always used to make me laugh, since his manager Herbie was the jazz man. Additionally, he loved to listen to soul music. His favourite song, 'You Make Me Feel Brand New,' was by the Stylistics. Although Peter did not talk about it much, he really loved R&B. He was very much into music by O.C. Smith who I think was his favourite R&B singer.

I would have also liked to see the books in Peter's personal library. From my conversations with him, I could tell that he read a lot of books.

The Reader
and Learner

by Desmond Shakespeare

Peter's affable, fun-loving personality is what I miss most about him. He was always a joy to be around because he was so entertaining. Even when he was being serious, you would end up laughing.

Prior to meeting Peter, I had always admired his music. However, I first met him by chance when he attended a concert at Excelsior High School in Jamaica – which is my alma mater. I just happened to be heading over to the event when we bumped into each other on campus. He needed directions to the school's auditorium and asked me for assistance. I told him that I was on my way there and we walked over to the building together. It turns out that he was at the function to lend his support to some of his peers who were scheduled to perform, whom he had recorded with at Studio One, while a member of the Wailers. En route to the auditorium, Peter remarked that I was the only person he had ever met who was taller than himself. I am six feet six inches in height while Peter was six feet two inches tall. When we arrived at the auditorium, we sat together.

Shortly thereafter, I went to the USA to further my education and lost touch with Peter. Upon returning to Jamaica, I renewed my ties with him through two mutual friends of ours, namely Barry Morais and Herbie Miller. Peter and I shared an interest in the struggles of oppressed people, particularly those of African descent. We had many conversations about this subject which helped to forge our friendship – one that would span approximately 13 years.

While our concern for the conditions of the downtrodden cemented our relationship, what I valued the most about our closeness was Peter's sense of fun. He was a great person to be around, and was always making some interesting statements, or cracking jokes. On the topic of jokes, in the 1970s, Peter owned a car which was plastered with decals of flags from different countries from around the world. One day I said to him, 'Peter, you have all these flags from different places, but I don't see the Jamaican flag. How come I don't see the Jamaican flag?' Peter replied, 'The Jamaican flag don't have red, green and gold inna it man!'

Another strong recollection that I have of Peter's razor-sharp wit is when he and I travelled together to Grenada in 1980. He had been invited by the then revolutionary government of Maurice Bishop to attend the commemoration of the first anniversary of the revolution. When we arrived at the airport, the person who had been sent to pick us up informed us that we could not depart just yet because the Prime Minister was en route to meet the former Prime Minister of Jamaica, Michael Manley, and the President of Nicaragua, Daniel Ortega. When Bishop arrived, we were introduced to him. In greeting Peter, Bishop said, 'Welcome, comrade!' To which Peter retorted, 'No! I don't come red. I come *black*.' I do not think that Bishop picked up on what Peter was saying because he just went on greeting the other delegates. Most likely his mind was on the two heads of state that were scheduled to arrive shortly.

While Peter was a riot, he took his music and the struggles of Africa and Africans, *very* seriously. When not preoccupied with such matters, I believe that animals, reading and marijuana were Peter's greatest passions. Sometimes when Herbie was away, he would ask me to pick Peter up at the airport when he was returning to Jamaica. On one occasion, Peter had smuggled into the island two rodents, which turned out to be hamsters, by hiding them in his shirt sleeves. Prior to this, I had never seen a hamster, and when we got in my car, Peter let them loose on my dashboard. I said to him, 'What is this?!' He replied, 'Don't worry man, them naw trouble yu. Don't worry.' He had them for quite some time as pets in his home.

From being around Peter, I came to realise that he kept abreast of current affairs, especially things that had to do with governments and how they dealt with people who are dispossessed. Peter was quite interested in such matters. He regularly listened to the news and also read a lot. I was impressed by the fact that Peter read. Before he and I became friends, I had no idea that he was a guy who read, let alone so avidly.

I believe that Peter's love of reading stemmed from his curiosity about certain subjects and that led to his desire to gain as much knowledge as he possibly could on them. From having grown up not far from where some Rastas lived on Wareika Hill, I know that some Rastas have a love of reading magazines and books about Africa. So, I suspect living in Trench Town could also have possibly sparked his interest in this hobby.

In terms of Peter's personal library, I recall that he had many books on cannabis. Before meeting Peter, I did not know that so many different strains of marijuana existed. He was really into exploring the topic of ganja and its various uses – what to do with the oil, the seed, and the whole plant. Peter would talk about the differences between Sensimilla, King's Bread, and Lamb's Bread, etc. I recall that he would even use the seeds when cooking certain dishes, but primarily used the seeds in baking. Once, he shared one of his pudding recipes with a female neighbour, who in turn sent it to the *Jamaica Gleaner* newspaper, which published it in their food section and had explained that she had gotten this recipe from Peter. He also used the oil from the seeds as an ointment for his skin.

On another occasion when I went to pick Peter up at the airport, he had three different books on marijuana, which he had acquired while on his travels. I said to him, 'Peter, what are you doing with more books on marijuana?' He replied, 'Bwoy, it's because you don't know.'

Peter took reading and book collecting seriously. That

being said, he did not collect books according to the names of authors, but instead, by subject matter. While his collection was not extensive, it was impressive. I remember that he owned a book about the travels of the Apostles throughout Europe after the crucifixion of Jesus. None of us knew how Peter came into possession of this book. I later discovered that it was some rare edition, of which only the British Museum had a copy. He would collect these special books and not disclose how he got them.

Although Peter towards the end of his life would speak frequently about ghosts and vampires, I never really saw much literature in his collection on that topic. His library was basically comprised of books and magazines about Africa and marijuana. From my visits to his home, I got the impression that Peter was the type of reader who read several books at a time, instead of starting and finishing one book before turning his attention to the next one.

Having been raised in a family where there was a lot of literature on Marcus Garvey and Africa, similar to Peter, I was quite knowledgeable about these subjects. Since we were both passionate about matters pertaining to Africa, whenever we would get together, our conversations usually revolved around black history and culture, and the struggles occurring in places like Mozambique, Angola, and then apartheid in South Africa. I remember once, an interviewer asked Peter, 'If you love Africa so much, with all that is going on there, would you die for Africa?' Peter replied, 'How yu mean die for Africa? If everybody dies for Africa, who is going to live for Africa?'

Despite the fact that Peter was always talking about Africa, evidently because it was one of the tenets of his Rastafari faith, I admired him for never putting down Jamaica. Wherever he went, he always spoke well about his homeland. I recall that in 1980, when there was a lot of political upheaval in Jamaica, Peter was in Houston, Texas and being interviewed on TV. The interviewer said to him, 'So, what's going on with the war in Jamaica?' Peter looked at him and said,

War? What war? I just a come from Jamaica and I don't

see any war down there. Jamaica is the nicest little place to be. What we have is a few misguided people shooting at each other, but there's no war down there.

Additionally, whenever Peter travelled abroad, he always looked forward to returning home.

Despite our differing backgrounds, Peter and I got along very well because we had a mutual respect for each other. On yet another visit to his house, when we talked about our favourite topics, he said to me, 'You know, you are a Rasta. You talk like a Rasta. You are a Rasta but you just don't say it.' People find this hard to believe, but despite his making that comment, and our years of friendship, Peter never once tried to convert me to Rasta, nor did he ever offer me marijuana. We genuinely understood and accepted each other's lifestyle.

...contrary to popular belief, Peter was always neatly dressed...

Most people in Jamaica are under the impression that Peter was this undisciplined 'Rasta Bwoy,' but contrary to popular belief, Peter was always neatly dressed and his shirt was always tucked in his pants. Sometimes when I would visit, he would be in the process of trimming his beard in front of a mirror.

In addition to taking pride in his personal appearance, Peter always kept his home clean. Furthermore, without exception, he had a fitness regime of swimming in the stream near his home in Ensom City in the mornings, doing martial arts, or riding his unicycle.

Moreover, despite the perception his stage persona may have given people, he was also very respectful of others' customs and culture. For example, while we were in Grenada, Peter was invited to perform at an indoor arena. After singing several songs at this event, which were well received by the audience, Peter proceeded to sit in the back of the assembly hall and watch the other performances. I recollect that a Jamaican drama group also performed a skit. While watching them, Peter struck up a conversation with a young lady and lit a spliff. A young Jamaican lady who was living and working in Grenada at the time, approached and informed me that, 'You need to tell Peter Tosh that although this is a revolutionary government, Grenadians do not really condone the smoking of ganja in public.' I turned to Peter and said to him in patois, 'Peter, bwoy, the people dem doan want yu smoke yu ganja in dem place yu know.' Which in standard English means that he must stop smoking his spliff because the Grenadians found his behaviour inappropriate in a public setting. Peter immediately extinguished his joint and remarked, 'Man, yu know when yu are in another man's house yu have to obey his rules, yu know.'

I suspect that Peter probably had felt comfortable lighting his spliff in the arena because two days earlier our assigned driver had taken us to a ganja field. There, the soldiers who were manning the field engaged in discourse with Peter about the cultivation of marijuana. Peter, naturally being in his element, proceeded to instruct them on the proper way to plant and grow cannabis.

I have one final comment on Peter the artist, who, prior to evolving into the performer, would give 'livatribes' during his set. He had, earlier in his career, performed without saying anything to the audience. This was the period before the One Love Peace Concert. I remember that one day during rehearsals, Herbie said to Peter, 'Yu know somethin' boss, you should engage your audience more. You should speak to them.' I too encouraged Peter to follow Herbie's advice. We would tell Peter that whenever there was a break in the band's set, he should utilise that time to speak. During rehearsals for the upcoming One Love Peace Concert, when the band took a break, we would ask Peter what he planned to say, and he would kiss his teeth and reply, 'Don't worry 'bout dat man. Me know exactly whey me a go seh.' Of course, no one believed that Peter was going to say anything. That all changed however, on the night of the concert. When he started his speech and said, 'This is not a peace concert, it is an integration concert.

All these people who are warring need to come together and integrate.' I said to myself, 'Oh my, he *really* has something to say.' Then he proceeded to talk about police brutality, and how such brutalisation affected the behaviour of our youth, plus his personal experiences with the police. This I thought was fine. Later, when he specifically addressed the politicians in attendance and began to lace his speech with profanity, I thought his language turned off many in the audience. Although what Peter was saying made a lot of sense, I felt that when he decided to accentuate his speech with obscenities, it detracted from all the good things he had mentioned. People were no longer concentrating on the substance of his message, instead, their focus was now on his delivery. Once he got started, I realised that he was going to go down a slippery slope, and I wished for him to quickly end his speech. Although I felt that he had gone beyond the bounds of good taste, I never broached the subject with him. That being said, when he showed me the lyrics to his controversial song, 'Bumbo Klaat!' I enquired why he felt the need to write it. He informed me that many people were curious about the meaning of these Jamaican expletives, so he was enlightening them. Interestingly enough, nowadays, this explicit song is very popular at parties.

Reflecting on Peter's life and personality, I believe that he would want to be remembered as someone who struggled for the rights of oppressed people. He was really fierce about that and truly challenged the system. Unfortunately, people view him as this undisciplined, ganja-smoking person. While this crafted image worked for his stage persona, in real life he was radically different.

*The Lion of Judah –
an important icon of
Tosh's Rastafarian faith.
Monument in Addis Ababa*
© Ondřej Žváček

The Lionhearted
Pioneer

by Herbie Miller

All things considered, Peter Tosh is still the most informed and articulate reggae musician that I have ever known, dealt with, or listened to. I first met Peter through the music of the Wailers in 1963, when their first big single, 'Simmer Down,' was released. I personally thought of and admired them as the greatest group of musicians that I was interested in at that time. They had a little corner shop in Kingston, located at 101 Orange Street, but the entrance to it was really on Beeston Street. One day while I went shopping there for records, I bumped into Peter. While he did not know me, I knew who he was, and since he was very friendly, he struck up a conversation with me.

Of the three Wailers, Peter was the easiest one to talk to because he had a very outgoing personality and would chat with everybody. He was initially responsible for bringing outsiders such as me into their circle. Most people only got to know the Wailers on a professional basis, but I was fortunate to also get to know them on a personal level. I feel extremely blessed to have known the primary three Wailers – especially Peter.

After Peter and I became friends, and he had completed the *Legalise It* recording and was preparing to go on his first solo tour as Peter Tosh in April or May 1976, I would pass around his place in Ensom City, near to Spanish Town, in the evenings after leaving my office at Kingston Wharves Ltd, and assist in any way that I could. Such assistance ran the gamut from getting the necessary items ready for their departure, to transporting musicians to his place, to giving someone a ride home and running some errands. On the night before Peter and his band were scheduled to depart for their Miami tour, I was at his home with a 'bredren' named 'Biggs'. Biggs was very close to Peter and served as his personal assistant and cook. After all the preparations had been made, Biggs said, 'Isn't Herbie coming with us?' I replied, 'No, I'm not going.' Biggs then turned to Peter and said, 'If Herbie isn't coming, who is going to look out for us?' Peter took US$200 out of his wallet, gave it to me and said, 'Join us in Miami.'

I loved to attend the Newport Jazz festival which was held in New York in June, and would always take my vacation to coincide with the time of that festival. Now, I had to go and hurriedly arrange my vacation. The thought then occurred to me that if I used my vacation to accompany them to Miami, I would not have enough vacation time remaining for the Newport Jazz festival. At that time, I had a very good job as a supervisor at the Kingston Wharves Ltd, which was comparable in pay and benefits to that of working at the bauxite company. It was an enviable job for any young man to have in the 1960s and is still so, even today. Since music is really my passion, I decided to take my chances with Peter and joined him and his band in Miami a few days later. That is how I came to work with and manage Peter. I would remain his manager until around late 1982, through the early part of 1983.

When I arrived in Miami, I met a man named Ted Camon, who was the manager of Miles Davis's drummer, Tony Williams. At this time, I also met a tour accountant named Bruce. I did not know anything about being a tour manager and they did not know anything about Jamaicans and Rastafari. Many other things baffled them after hanging out for several days with these guys, such as their speech, and them never being on time. Nothing was achieved, except for Peter wanting to go to health food stores, his wanting a stove and other items. So, a meeting was held in Ted's room, at which time I realised that he was Tony Williams's manager, as Tony was also present.

Bruce and Ted taught me everything they could for the duration of that tour and this created a bond between us. It was not a long tour – some of the shows were cancelled – but I clearly remember us doing shows at the Beacon Theatre in New York, Harvard University in Boston, and the University of Miami in Coral Gables.

Although Peter did not have the focused work ethic that I associate with the late Bob Marley, he did not take his music lightly. Similar to Miles Davis, Peter did not arrive at the studio with his music fully developed. He conceived the bones of the composition in his mind and then communicated it to his band by playing it and had them extend his idea. He knew in his mind where he wanted it to go, and was able to maintain spontaneity and freshness by not strictly assigning to his musicians the roles that he wanted them to play. He was democratic in how he made his music because he knew that he had a great band. From his sketch, his band members could incorporate their own sense of creativity and develop the composition.

He was happiest performing live.

While some people felt that Peter was not really prepared for work, I disagreed. Let us take for instance, Joe Higgs's song 'Steppin' Razor,' which he had recorded earlier for Studio One. I, without knowing that Higgs wrote the original version, assumed that Peter had written the song and assigned authorship to him. When Higgs asserted ownership of the lyrics, Peter immediately verified his claim and assigned him the rights to the song. However, if you listen to 'Steppin' Razor' as recorded on the *Equal Rights* album it will be abundantly clear that what was written by Higgs and recorded by Peter earlier was different. You will hear additional lyrics on Peter's production, which had transformed the original into a fuller composition. Therefore, Peter could easily have claimed co-authorship.

I admired the way he allowed his musicians to express themselves freely – they were not restricted. Robbie Shakespeare, Sly Dunbar, and Mikey Chung are all outstanding musicians. When one has two lead guitarists like Al Anderson and Donald Kinsey, or Daryl Thompson, their ability to improvise must be encouraged. Peter allowed them all the freedom to express themselves. When you listen to the *Bush Doctor* and *Mystic Man* albums, you can hear the level of musical arrangement that Peter did and can see that it made sense. It is only logical that the music would grow in the direction it did. Peter would only exercise his leadership when he was dissatisfied with some of what his musicians offered, and when he reached that point, he would be honest and tell them that he did not want them to do X, Y, or Z. He was a great band leader.

Peter's democratic style was best exemplified when he was on the stage. He was happiest performing live. If you look at his performances, you can see he was really having a good time. He is looking back at his band members smiling, he is having fun just hugging his guitar and watching them. He is having fun playing those great riffs that I credit him with introducing to reggae music. The texture, the rapidity, the multiplicity of the reggae stroking – it was not just chaka-chaka-chaka. It was chukuchuku-chukuchuku-chukuchuku-chuk chuk chuk chuk. Chuk, chuk, chuk, chuk! The ways he used the clavinet sound, the sound of the wah-wah riffs, and the textures that he brought to the sound, some musicians playing today do not realise that many of the methods they use were invented by him.

His sense of musicality, his ability to pick up different instruments and in a couple of days be proficient at playing them, greatly impressed me. For instance, when Peter did 'Creation,' he was playing a harp. He had stepped into a pawn shop and saw this harp. He picked it up, started strumming it, and liked it, so he bought it. A few months later, he came to my house and gave me this track for 'Creation.' He is just singing and playing to the accompaniment of this harp and that's what 'Creation' is. No big set of instruments – it was just Peter, his harp, and acoustic guitar.

When I met Peter as an artist, he was already a professional. However, when he collaborated with the Rolling Stones, it allowed me to see his growth at a very high level. He worked with some of the best in the business. Observing what they brought and how they elevated performances from something flat to something quite magical was enlightening. Although I was not a performer, I too learned a lot from the Stones and was able to encourage, convey, and inspire that vibe in the guys.

I remember once that Peter and his band were going to perform at a famed rock club on Long Island called My Father's Place, run by Michael 'Eppy' Epstein. Whenever Peter was in town, Eppy did everything that he could to assist him with playing at his club. I recall one particular show that was held on a Sunday. In those days, with the exception of Sly who was always singular-minded in how he dressed, and remains so to this day, the other band members liked to perform in sweat suits as if they were athletes. This was also the case with all other reggae artists. I decided to go to a store that sold Indian apparel and purchased the long cotton shirts that the men wear called kurta and a few of the baggy trousers called dhotis. Robbie, who was one of the main culprits of the sweat suit style, tried on the outfit. He took one look at himself in the mirror, and then took it off claiming that it made him look like a girl. So, it was back to the sweat suits. It was on that tour that they started to realise the importance of colours, attire, and the need to look different from everybody else.

At this time, they also learned how to use the stage effectively. Previously, they would all huddle in one small section of the stage. Peter back then was a flat-footed performer who would stand there hugging his little wah-wah guitar, with one foot on the wah-wah pedal and the other over the microphone. Robbie and I decided to take away Peter's guitar and his wah-wah, and encourage him to have fun using the entire stage. Naturally, Peter let us have it. Robbie and Sly then developed a little routine where Sly would use his drumsticks to hit on the bass strings while Robbie would control the notes on the bass when Sly was hitting it.

Similarly, Keith and Mick of the Rolling Stones had this rapport where they would pay a lot of attention to each other, with Keith going out front and being right in Mick's face and they would really have a great time on stage with each other. Robbie, to a certain extent, adopted that style when in the position of the lead guitar player. He would have fun getting close to his partner, and sharing the microphone.

Peter had a pioneering spirit which I greatly admired. As far as I am concerned, Peter and his band were the first in the world to use cordless equipment which was called NASTY at the time. The technology had been developed by a bunch of guys who wanted the Stones to use it. I recall that the Stones used the equipment during their rehearsals while we used the standard gear, but I believe that they were a little hesitant to use the equipment because their productions were on such a high level they did not want to be the guinea pigs. They did not want everything to go quiet in the middle of a performance. So, since Peter was open to innovative things, we ended up using the equipment. This is another quality of his that I admired – his fearlessness of technology and willingness to change. The effect this had on our shows was amazing! One could now hear when Peter started singing in the dressing room, but could not see him. So, when the audience was looking all over the place for him, he would walk out on stage singing, and people would say, 'Oh my God! Where is the microphone?'

To my knowledge, Peter was one of the first artists whose work employed digital video technology in 1977 or 1978. You

Peter had a pioneering spirit...was open to innovative things

Miller and Tosh, Music Fair,
Little Premier Plaza, Kingston,
Jamaica, 1977
© Avrom Robin/Susan Finkelstein

could see four of the same images fusing into one, and conversely, one into multiples. As an aside, I recall that on one occasion Peter had purchased a watch which greatly fascinated him. On the face of the watch all he had to do was touch a little button and it did what he wanted it to do. This was very early digital technology not yet developed that really intrigued him.

In terms of Peter's fight against injustice and oppression, it is readily identifiable in his stage outfits and props. His karate gi outfits, the nunchaku, the sword, and handcuffs that he had added to his arsenal so to speak, were both personal martial arts material and statements against Babylon.

Peter was one of the first artists whose work employed digital video technology

Regarding his practice of martial arts, he preferred to call it African martial arts. There was once a TV series in Jamaica called *Kung Fu* which depicted martial arts at its deepest, meditative form – not considering the act of the arts itself in self-defense. Kung Fu interested Peter because it unified the mind, body, and self-defense. The primary reasons for Peter practising it were on account of the meditative aspect of this art form, the deep inner search, the balance and the calm that it engenders, plus the act of self-defense that one develops.

When Peter would integrate roundhouse kicks, chops, and punches in his stage performances, they were done on the spur of the moment and were also statements of resistance against Babylon. None of his actions were choreographed. It was basically how he wanted to express himself at that particular time. Peter was extremely agile and his body could do a lot of things. With his frame, he looked like a ballet dancer would look doing a high kick. To see a man of that height do a high kick was very elegant.

Peter was unafraid of controversy. I recall during the Madison Square Garden show in 1977, Peter bought himself a traditional long, ankle-length jillaba or dishdasa, with a keffiyeh and agal headgear, similar to that worn by Arab men of the Gulf region, and performed in it. He intentionally did this at the No Nukes concert because he knew that there were certain countries with nuclear armaments and the concert date also fell close to one of the Jewish holidays. He made this political statement fully aware that there were still ongoing conflicts between the Arab and Jewish states in the Middle East.

In the late 1970s, Peter's position as a highly influential figure is best evidenced by his being the first reggae artist invited to address the UN committee on the issue of apartheid. I do not know why or how the event was cancelled, but the invitation was rescinded after his performance at the No Nukes concert.

Being very vocal, Peter's decision to speak out against apartheid also meant that he had to make hard decisions. Peter was approached by an African American acting on the behalf of a South African beer company, to perform in South Africa. This invitation was extended shortly after Steven Biko's death. The beer company made Peter numerous lucrative financial offers, but he declined all of them. He and I were very clear that was not what we wanted to do. We then met with the South African jazz musician named 'Dollar Brand,' who later performed as Abdullah Ibrahim. We visited him one evening to discuss apartheid and he was very instrumental in helping us to understand it.

In addition to being a trailblazer in technology and political activism, Peter was also the first reggae artist to perform in Italy. I had a personal interest in Italy because the other type of music that I like is jazz and some of my favourite jazz musicians were performing in Italy during this era. This was interesting because the political climate in Italy at that time was unstable and many other artists avoided playing there during that period.

Another quality of Peter's that I admired was his sense of adventure. He always took chances. I recall that on one occasion we were stranded in the US Virgin Islands on the island of St Thomas and we ended up having to charter some little Cessna to transport us to another island. Peter was sitting beside the pilot, while Robbie and I were in the back. Both Robbie and I were scared. Peter then touched an instrument on the dashboard and Robbie got on his case. Those are the kinds of things that Peter would do. I am sure that if the pilot would have allowed him to fly the aircraft, he would have attempted to do so.

On the topic of flying, Peter was enchanted by the idea of man flying. By this, I mean man's ability to literally fly. He believed that ancient dreads could fly. In his music, Peter reveals his fascination with flying and also a lot about himself, but people were not listening carefully. Two songs that come to mind are, '(If I Had the) Wings of a Dove' and 'Pick Myself Up.' He also did interviews in which he spoke about the concept of man flying.

...was enchanted by the idea of man flying.

Initially, when Peter broached the topic I laughed, but when we were staying on the twentieth-plus floor of a hotel in Ipanema and some people stopped by to hang out with us and he talked about men flying back to Africa and the new world, then started walking towards the open window as if to prove his point, I realised that he was serious. With Dermot Hussey, who was also in the room, I suggested to Peter that he did not have to prove to us then that concept of men being able to fly.

While researching the topic, I later discovered that idea of flying was prevalent among certain enslaved saltwater Africans who flew back and forth to Africa. There were cases of some slaves even killing themselves because they believed that it was the spirit that flew back and morphed into the person again once they got back. There are historic narratives available from historians like Michael A. Gomez, who wrote 'A Quality of Anguish: The Igbo Response to Enslavement in the Americas,' plus WPA papers that discuss this phenomenon. Now that I have more knowledge about this concept, I am pretty confident about my ability to defend it. I do not view it as being any different from the concept of the Resurrection morning that we all are expecting.

On a lighter note, I found Peter's sense of adventure, as evidenced by some of his hobbies, and ability to be a 'big kid' at heart, amusing. In 1977, Peter discovered unicycling as a hobby. He was passing a bicycle shop and saw this long bicycle with two wheels, low, like a sports car that one can recline in. He was initially interested in buying it, but thought that because of its length, it would be too cumbersome to travel around with, so he ended up buying a unicycle instead. In a short time, he had taught himself and mastered riding his unicycle.

Once while performing in California, Bill Graham threw Peter's unicycle off the stage. At that time, Peter was touring with the Rolling Stones and Graham did not know who he was, so when Peter came on stage riding his unicycle, Graham threw him off. Afterwards, the unicycle became one of Peter's stage props.

Prior to his interest in unicycles, Peter rode skateboards. I recall that many times he fell flat on his butt inside some airport because he decided to ride his skateboard through the facility before mastering balance. Even before learning how to ride a skateboard, Peter was into roller-skating. He also loved toys and had a room full of objects. Someone once remarked to me that since Peter did not have any toys as a child, he probably was trying to compensate for the childhood he never had by buying all these toys for himself. Plus he had motorboats, airplanes, racing cars, slingshots, and other little objects.

In addition to playing with his toys, Peter likewise enjoyed watching TV programmes such as the Hanna Barbera cartoons productions of *Heckle and Jeckle*, and *Mr. Magoo*. While Peter enjoyed animations, he also watched serious programmes such as the news. He never missed the news broadcast if he could help it. Furthermore, he loved to watch vampire and ghost movies. This led him to identify certain people in society as such, and when he did his song, 'Vampire,' he was referring to those individuals. It was very interesting to note that the ghosts and vampires would haunt him whenever he was driving his automobile. Peter drove very fast and would crash his car regularly, then blame it on the ghosts and vampires.

Another of his hobbies was reading. Peter loved to read the Bible, literature about the origins of the apartheid system, (we each bought a book in Brussels called *The Brotherhood*, which discussed the South African leaders' involvement in the system) and biographies on African leaders and Pan-Africanists such as Marcus Garvey, Walter Rodney, and Malcolm X. It was actually this mutual interest in politics and world affairs that bonded Peter and I together. We were the only ones in the group who were political. Back then, many of our peers were apolitical and unfamiliar with apartheid. It was this era of legal segregation and political unrest that inspired Peter's recording of the album *Equal Rights*.

Peter also loved animals – all kinds – and had a yard full of weird creatures. I recall that on one occasion, he smuggled into Jamaica what appeared to have been a pair of hamsters. It turned out that they were two males, and eventually, one of them castrated the other.

While we were on tour in Europe, we encountered an organ grinder with a chimpanzee in Switzerland. When Peter saw the chimp, he thought that he should get one to bring back to his home in Jamaica. Peter immediately tried to bond with the ape, but for some reason, it had no interest in him and was trying to escape him. Peter kept on pursuing the chimp and when it had reached its limit, it finally boxed him. Peter looked at the ape in disbelief! Not wanting the chimp to have one box up on him, Peter then chased it, until the opportunity arose for him to slap it back.

When Peter was not performing, I think that he enjoyed being home in Jamaica most, driving through the countryside to check his bredren, his bush doctor, and buy his bush. While travelling with Peter, I observed that he had set ideas about doing certain activities, such as building a spliff while driving. On one occasion, we were driving down Constant Spring Road in Jamaica with a couple of music executives who Peter had a contract with. Peter had a way of steering the car with his knees while he built a spliff, driving at about 70 mph. He would do these crazy manoeuvres with his knees, which none of us liked, but he assured us that he could handle it and everything was alright. He built his spliff, lit it, and then passed it around. One of the passengers took a couple of puffs before passing it to the next person. That man did the same and passed it to me, but I was not a smoker. I know that I should not give it to Peter, who was at this time, rolling another spliff, so I passed it back to the guy who gave it to me, and he in turn, returned it to the first passenger. That man tried to give it to Peter who stated, 'No man, that is yours. In Jamaica, every man smokes his own spliff.'

A story about Peter is incomplete if his keen wit is not mentioned. When it comes to having a sense of humour, Peter had it. He was very witty, perceptive, and had great timing with delivering his punch lines. One of my strongest recollections of his wisecracks is a tale about the rock band, the Grateful Dead. It was the end of 1977, when we toured with the Rolling Stones in New York. The Grateful Dead was also there for a three or four night engagement. Daily, they would call to invite Peter to attend one of their shows. They were willing to roll out the red carpet for him. Due to exhaustion from our daily activities, by nighttime, we were very tired. Lou Rawls was also in town and Peter really wanted to see him perform, but was too exhausted to go. The day of the night of our final performance, the telephone rang and Peter answered it. The caller invites Peter to attend the Grateful Dead's show and says, 'We really want you to come. We'll send a car for you. You will get the red carpet treatment.' Peter enquired, 'What's the name of the band?' The caller replied, 'The Grateful Dead.' Peter, in his whimsical, playful, humourous, cheeky way, instantly responded, 'You guys should be grateful to be alive.' Needless to say, although Peter promised to attend their show, due to exhaustion, he was unable to keep his promise.

Furthermore, Peter was not overly sensitive and could take good-natured ribbing. He always loved to shop on 'Cheap Street.' By that he meant that he did not shop at places that sold expensive things. He would shop on Delancey Street in New York City where he would buy half a dozen or more of the same items. Robbie and I used to tease him that since he bought cheap stuff, by the time he returned to the hotel, the object would have stopped working, so he would need to replace it with a new one.

Jamaica belatedly acknowledged the contribution of Peter Tosh to the country's musical development and culture.

Humour aside, when reflecting on Peter's professional achievements, I am most impressed by his *Equal Rights* recording. That is because on that recording he introduced to the world the whole evil and reality of the apartheid system, which was supported by all of the 'First World' countries. Not one country was opposed to apartheid. Peter as a high profile performer brought that consciousness to the world. It meant that he was also invited to perform at anti-apartheid concerts both in Europe and the USA. He did these shows without ever charging any money.

Peter was one of the innovators and one of the first persons to take our music to every corner of this earth. We have reached a point in Jamaica where we no longer consider the Wailers as a group. So today, we hardly hear music by Bunny Wailer, and sadly, none by Peter Tosh. Peter was one of the innovators and one of the first persons to take our music to every corner of this earth. We have reached a point in Jamaica where we no longer consider the Wailers as a group. So today, we hardly hear music by Bunny Wailer, and sadly, none by Peter Tosh. I find that very disappointing. In my opinion, he was not acknowledged to the degree that I believe he should have been and the reason for that is because his music was uncompromisingly truthful. Since people cannot find ways to water it down, it has been rejected. On a positive note, Irie FM radio station in February 2011 saw it fit to honour Peter; and through recommendations and lobbying, Jamaica belatedly acknowledged the contribution of Peter Tosh to the country's musical development and culture. In August 2012, 25 years after his death, Winston Hubert McIntosh aka Peter Tosh was appointed a member of the Order of Merit (OM), receiving the country's third highest national honour.

While Peter's legacy in his homeland has waned, internationally he is respected. I am always amazed by the number of emails I receive from Europeans and Africans after I have written a piece on Peter, expressing their admiration of him. I recall on one of our tours to Holland in 1978, a small group of fans came out to greet us when we landed at the airport. There was a surgeon in their midst. He introduced himself to me and said that he was a doctor; he saves people's lives, but ironically, he was unable to save those of his family who died in a plane crash. He was supposed to have joined them on vacation. He confided that he had been depressed and contemplated suicide. While lying on his bed, Peter's song, 'Pick Myself Up,' came on the radio, and it inspired him to live and help others live. He gave me a little turtle carved in stone, which symbolises long life. I still have that turtle, sitting on the edge of my bathtub. His gift illustrates to me the kind of impact that Peter's music and that of other great reggae artists like Bunny, Bob, and Jimmy Cliff have on people around the world.

Two other strong recollections that I have of Peter, which illustrate his far-reaching influence, concern those who were also involved in the fight for justice. One night while performing at the Loose Caboose in Dallas, Texas, there was a terrible storm. Peter and the band had just finished their show when the security officer on duty, a man named Slim (I swear that he was 7 feet tall!) informed us that some folks who drove all the way from Houston, Texas to be there tonight were at the door. It was now 1:00 a.m. and Slim then handed me a card from the latecomers. When I read it, I saw that it was from Kwame Ture (the late Stokely Carmichael). I said, 'Of course, let them in!' Ture and his friends had packed into a VW Beetle and travelled quite a distance in the storm to meet Peter.

On another occasion, it brought me great pleasure to quietly witness the exchange that occurred between Peter and Angela Davis when they met in the early 1980s, at the Greek Theatre in Los Angeles. Here were two freedom fighters, male and female, united in the struggle. That is the kind of impact that Peter had on others who were also involved with the cause.

In retrospect, the thing that I am most grateful for about my relationship with Peter was that he put that US$200 in my pocket and told me to join him in Miami. Due to Peter, my path in life took a different direction and I have not regretted it. I had an exciting and adventurous life. I saw the world, was exposed to it, and was able to see humanity in a way that I could not have seen it if I had remained trapped in Jamaica. I also had the opportunity to experience a new way of life, one that I would never have known if I had stayed on at the Wharves. I travelled the world and was exposed to many different people and languages. These experiences helped me to grow and better understand people that I meet at every level of society. To have lifelong friendships with such individuals is very humbling. From the man on the street who is hustling secondhand books about Garvey and is very knowledgeable about the contents of such books, to interacting with the Julian Bonds of the world, and playing a role in giving all of them the rallying cry of 'Get Up, Stand Up!' is very gratifying. If it was not for Peter, I would not be who I am today. So, even in a moment of what I would like to think of as misguided influence, when Peter fired me, although it hurt, I put it behind me and, instead, cherished the opportunities that he gave me.

On the Road
with a Reggae Radical

by Jayne Cortez

Peter Tosh was very supportive of and committed to Pan-African struggles. He was assertive and revolution was within his work. His weapons were his words and music, and his words encouraged people who were in politics to be revolutionaries. He sang about black life, oppression, liberation and dreams.

Peter combined his political interest with his music. Reggae was a relatively new form at that time, so the combination of Peter's political concerns mixed with reggae was significant. One of the problems that artists and entertainers have is that their artistic concerns don't always mesh. They are not always able to put those two things together and the timing is not always right. In Peter's case, the timing was good because it was the period of hyper-civil rights/black power activity in the USA, and it was the period of hyperactivity in the Southern African liberation movements.

As an artist myself, it was nice to know that someone else had an interest in similar subjects and topics. The impact of our synergy was a corroboration of creative possibilities. Peter was very serious, very sensitive, his communication skills were excellent, and he was a dynamic singer/composer/ musician/ performer. The beat was steady, but what he placed on top or behind the beat was how he related to that beat, to the musicians, and the body movements of dancers; that placement was not always predictable.

In the winter of 1979, bass player Richard Davis's and my path crossed with Peter's when we were the opening act for his Midwestern shows. Peter's manager, Herbie Miller, knew

Richard and about our Strata-East recording, *Celebrations and Solitudes*, so we agreed to open for Peter's band. From our collaboration, it was apparent that Peter clearly had the ability to perform and communicate well with two kinds of audiences – the general audience of a big city like Chicago and the student audience in Madison, Wisconsin. From my own experience, I know that's not easy. For Richard and me, this Chicago audience was different. Even though Richard grew up in Chicago, we were used to performing for audiences interested in black and avant-garde literature and the African American modern music known as 'jazz.'

Looking back on those events decades later gives me great joy. We were happy to have the opportunity to be the act opening for Peter. It was a wonderful experience that gave people two kinds of approaches to creative art and politics, two different approaches to words and music. This unusual and thoughtful combination enhanced ideas and developments, deepening the dialogue in Chicago and Madison in 1979. The way the material was organised, one could hear the history of black music, culture, language, and attitude, and feel the groove pulse articulated in the tune, or in spontaneous improvisations.

While on the bus going from Chicago to Madison I had the opportunity to observe the Word, Sound and Power band reading political books and discussing current events. I also discovered that Peter was not only a quiet person, but also a man with a great sense of humour. My encounters with Peter, the situation, and environment, inspired me to write the following three poems: 'Opening Act,' 'Black Feathered Mules,' and 'Milwaukee.' This was one of the coldest winters in North America. The snow was piled as high as the Blue Mountains in Jamaica, and here were Peter Tosh and his group heating up the cold and melting the snow.

'We Got to Come Together'

by Dr Omar Davies, MP

Although many people think of me as being mainly a Peter Tosh fan, the fact is that I am indeed a fan of the trio, initially as the original Wailers, and subsequently as solo artists. When The Wailers made their first US tour to promote the Island Records albums, *Catch a Fire* and *Burnin'*, I was teaching at Stanford University. One night while they were playing at a small club in San Francisco, my wife and I, together with a few friends, including Michael Witter, went to one of their shows. Bunny had refused to make the tour, the first sign of the imminent breakup of the group, and his place was taken by Joe Higgs.

Following the performance, I spent the rest of the night speaking with Tosh and was amazed at his range of interests. In particular, I was intrigued by his interest in world affairs, which he followed by listening to the BBC. During our conversation, Tosh mentioned that he planned to leave The Wailers. I recall him saying, 'There are too many flowers growing in my musical garden for me to continue playing second fiddle to any man.' Furthermore, he confided that Eric Clapton had invited him to join his band, but he declined that offer for the same reason. We had a lengthy discussion about his career aspirations, and later corresponded by mail for a period.

When I presented one of the first public analyses of Tosh's work at the University of the West Indies, it was under the banner of the Annual Bob Marley Lecture. I deliberately used the occasion to focus on Tosh's work because I was struck by the fact that there was too little public appreciation of his contribution to the development of Jamaica's pop music.

While it is true that there are a few who laud Tosh's significant contributions to the music, I believe that he is given little attention, relative to that accorded Marley, because of the sustained public relations drive initiated by Chris Blackwell (the former owner of Island Records) during the 1970s. That drive made Marley into an international superstar and is one of the reasons that he is bigger in death than he was in life. While Marley's legacy continues to be safeguarded, a similar initiative has not been undertaken with regard to Tosh's work. A concerted effort is needed to keep Tosh's legacy going.

There is a tendency by many foreigners, to define reggae almost solely in terms of Marley's work. As such, the prolonged promotion of the Marley brand has made it difficult for other performers (including Tosh, John Holt, the late Dennis Brown, or even more recently Buju Banton and Beres Hammond) to attain anything near to Marley's commercial success. One result is that there is a lack of full recognition of the contributions of many other artists to the development of reggae.

Now, focusing specifically on Tosh and his status in the eyes of his compatriots, while his boldness in speaking the truth in his music and his outspokenness in general are appreciated, collectively Jamaicans have not accorded him the same level of honour bestowed on Marley for three reasons:

a. His use of profanity

b. His advocacy for legalising marijuana

c. His confrontations with the police

Almost a quarter of a century later, these factors still bear heavily in terms of our assessment of him.

Although Tosh was much more articulate than Marley and did not pull any punches, I believe that many people were turned off by his liberal use of expletives. For example, my wife and I both admired Tosh because of his music as well as the fact that he was such an exciting performer. One never knew what to expect! He would ride his unicycle on stage, wear unique outfits, etc. However, his song, laced with Jamaican obscenities entitled, 'Bumbo Klaat!' is not played in our home.

Peter Tosh and Bob Marley, live at the
Matrix on Broadway, San Francisco,
October 29, 1973
© Chuck Krall Still Photographs

While it is a beautifully arranged composition, it is hard to comprehend why he chose to put such lyrics to it.

I suspect that Tosh saw it as his duty to take on the society and he objected to the notion that a set of meaningless words, ordained by the colonial Establishment as 'bad,' should continue to be judged to be unlawful. As far as he was concerned, such conformity indicated that we are still enslaved. While that may be the case, Jamaicans are at heart, a relatively conservative people.

It is for this same reason that many in attendance at the historic One Love Peace Concert deemed his use of profanity throughout his performance objectionable. I came away from the event wondering why he would use the occasion to give that spiel with the world watching. The segment of his speech directed at the Prime Minister and Leader of the Opposition was particularly troubling to many. While they have their faults, they were still our leaders and one does not berate them in such a public manner. Then to top it all off, Tosh brandished, lit, and smoked a spliff in their presence.

...the public did not find Tosh's rebellious nature endearing...

This approach was in contrast to Marley who also smoked herb and paid homage to it in several of his songs, like 'Kaya,' but never took on the Establishment frontally. Tosh not only wrote about marijuana, but would also smoke it in public places, getting into confrontations with the security forces. His refusal to back down or to put a façade on his views is also a critical element in the Jamaican public's assessment of him. One may argue that many of us, by being part of the status quo routinely do, or say, that which is 'politically correct.' However, I would not say that the Jamaican public has been overly harsh in its assessment of Tosh's behaviour. While he was an iconic figure, I do not believe that he went out of his way to be sensitive about the feelings of the general public. Unlike Marley who always seemed to be smiling and was never involved in civil disobedience, the public did not find Tosh's rebellious nature endearing.

Another source of contention is the perceived resentment some Jamaicans feel that Tosh had over Marley's commercial success. He objected vehemently to the billing of 'Bob Marley and the Wailers.' It is my understanding that Marley, Tosh, and Wailer had made a pact always to be together, so when the decision was made to market the group as Bob Marley and the Wailers, Tosh resented being seen as one of Marley's backup singers. After Marley's death, some comments made by Tosh about his late colleague were viewed as dismissive and negatively impacted on his standing in the eyes of some people.

Many individuals have asked me how I, as a politician, and as such a part of the status quo, viewed Tosh's anti-Establishment sentiments and blatant acts of defiance. I begin by indicating that I have always been troubled by the inequalities in our socio-economic system. Although the issues change with time, there will always be the need for oppressed people to oppose aspects of the prevailing system. In the past, the cry was against the existing colonial structure. While we have gained political independence, blatant inequalities remain in our justice and education systems. So, while issues may change in terms of topicality, the inequalities are always there, not only in Jamaica, but also elsewhere in the world.

Having witnessed firsthand the remaining inequalities in the Jamaican society, I spend a lot of time and energy in my constituency attempting to lift educational standards of the majority of residents. While some progress has been made, the harsh reality is that when students from the lowest income households reach the tertiary level, they continue to face challenges in getting to school, in obtaining textbooks, or eating regularly. This reality makes me realise how unfair the obstacles are which such students have to conquer. It is for this reason that I am always involved with initiatives that will help promote positive change and equity, and at the same time am supportive of similar positions from others, including musicians.

I derive relief from some of the injustice inherent in our society via the Arts – particularly music. During periods of despair, my favourite song to listen to is Tosh's 'Jah Seh No' from his *Mystic Man* album. I like to play that song because it gives me great solace and optimism that I can bear any trial that comes my way. Tosh's ability to take the most complex issue and articulate it effectively in music was incredible. When one considers his decision in 1977 to put all of his creative energies into producing an entire album in the fight against apartheid, a musician going against all trends, one must agree that was an amazing achievement on his part. His *Equal Rights* album is one of the finest I have ever heard.

Tosh's ability to take the most complex issue and articulate it effectively in music was incredible

The link between Tosh's work and his religious belief is also important for understanding him. In another article 'The Wailers: Giving Thanks and Praise,' published in the *Jamaica Journal*, April 2004, I analyse the Wailers' music as religion, and their religion as expressed in their music. I was motivated to write this essay after listening to hours of Tosh's music and realising the extent to which he had articulated his Rasta theology through his compositions.

Without a doubt, Tosh's body of work is a critical contribution to Jamaica's national identity, particularly in terms of developments in the latter part of the 1960s and the 1970s. Currently, there appears to be a superficial acclamation of our artists from the status quo. My hope is that future Administrations will promote the Arts in a more systematic manner, ensuring greater opportunities for the development of the musical talent of our youngsters. I believe that there should be formal studies of the work of Tosh and other outstanding artists, so that we may get to understand their viewpoints and more fully recognise their contributions. This however, cannot come about without cooperation between the music industry and the general public. The music industry needs to play its part in advising its members that if they wish to be taken seriously, they must conduct themselves in such a fashion that the public will regard them as professionals.

While several of our artists are 'rebels without a cause,' many of them have valid reasons for expressing their anti-Establishment views. By the same token, I would like artists to realise that the status quo is not wholly evil. In listening to Tosh's last song, 'We Got to Come Together,' on his final album, *No Nuclear War*, I wonder if he had reached a point in his life where he was seeking a middle ground.

Photographic
Profiles of Peter

by Chuck Krall

Peter was quite a colourful character! He was a very comical guy, and could have been in Cirque du Soleil. He had that kind of a personality. I remember at airports when he got bored, he would pull out his unicycle and ride it through the facility. Peter had a very high opinion of himself and so did I. He did not take a back seat to anyone and was not afraid of anyone. He thought of himself as an ambassador and loved to pontificate about how the world could be saved, but did not talk down to others. Although Peter never said so, I always felt that he thought he was not a mere mortal, that he was on a higher plane of knowledge. Peter was also compassionate and a very honest man. He was kind of like a brother to me.

I first met Peter with The Wailers in 1973, in San Francisco. Then, The Wailers were Bob Marley, Peter Tosh, Joe Higgs, a guy named Earl 'Wia' Lindo, and the Barrett brothers. To my knowledge, this was The Wailers' first time in the USA. They were on a west coast tour and in town for a show at the Matrix. The Wailers were staying at a motel on Lombard Street. I arrived early for a photo session, got to talking with Peter and that's how we became friendly. I liked him immediately!

His domestic partner, Yvonne Whittingham, cut me a large piece of Christmas melon and I offered him a bite. He said, 'Thank you,' and then walked off with the melon. I just stood there looking at him. Later, he returned laughing and gave me a copy of his 45, 'Can't Blame the Youth.' This was a real compliment to me because Peter thought that I would understand and like it.

Peter Tosh at a motel on Lombard Street,
San Francisco, October 30, 1973
© *Chuck Krall Still Photographs*

Peter Tosh and Yvonne Whittingham, at a motel on Lombard Street, San Francisco, October 30, 1973
© *Chuck Krall Still Photographs*

He knew of me when I was a Peace Corps volunteer in Jamaica in 1968, so we did not need any major introductions. At that time, I met Bob Marley and Joe Higgs in Trench Town. My first year, I was assigned to the Whitehouse Fishing Beach in Westmoreland near Bluefields, which was probably the most prolific as far as supplying fish to the hotels, so it was a really good place to be stationed. Later, I lived in Port Royal for another year, where I met a lot of interesting people.

In the motel room, someone asked for a cigarette and from living in Jamaica, I knew to break it open and mix the herb with tobacco. Since I knew how to do that, that mystified them and we got to talking. They liked the idea that I had lived in Jamaica, and Chris Blackwell wanted me to tour with them. So, since I was accepted, I travelled around with them for five years.

Even though I am Jewish, there were some similarities between Peter and myself. For example, we did not eat pork, or drink alcohol, and we loved to smoke herb. Peter and I had fun hanging out with each other because we both shared the same sense of humour and were comfortable with each other.

I had a positive experience working with Peter. He was very photogenic, tall, and good-looking, so I did not have any problem taking images of him. I never asked him to pose and only took pictures of him when something was worth shooting. We were comfortable with that arrangement.

My most interesting assignment of taking photos of Peter occurred around the time he did 'Don't Look Back' with Mick Jagger of the Rolling Stones. He was playing at the Roxy in Los Angeles and was at the height of his musical success. At that time, he had done many interviews and shows in Los Angeles, seemed to be at his most prosperous on a financial level, and was also a little less humble and more braggadocios. I remember that he did not seem to be on a budget then, like other musicians.

Another assignment of note was the Bob Marley concert at the Starlight Bowl Amphitheater in Burbank, California, in 1978. There, Peter joined Bob on stage for an unplanned duo. I

Bob Marley and Peter Tosh performing at the Starlight Amphitheatre
© Chuck Krall Still Photographs

was approximately 50 feet from the stage behind some bushes because that's the way the Amphitheater was set up, and I could not get on the stage. Every time I shot the flash, I was waiting 10 or 11 seconds for it to recycle before I could take another picture. It was not a concert that I recall as being very enjoyable. The sound system was too loud, and some people who had come with children were leaving before the end of the show because the volume hurt their ears. Peter came up from behind and just grabbed the microphone from Bob during their anthem 'Get Up, Stand Up.' It was funny! Nobody knew that Peter was in town, so we were all surprised to see him.

His herb was an extension of himself and not just a general commitment.

Bob and Peter had not spoken since around 1975. The series of images I took that night of Peter and Bob together turned out well, but I had to do a lot of work and corrections to get some of them looking good.

My favourite images of Peter are the ones of him smoking herb. I have a lot of pictures of Peter on stage, smoking right in front of the audience, or rolling his spliff. He made the biggest spliffs! I am most fond of those pictures because they were so intimate and reminded me of a special moment. As a policy, I never photographed musicians with any kind of drugs. When I was with Jimi Hendrix, Janis Joplin and other big time artists, and the drugs came out, I put my camera away. In Peter's case, it was different because the herb was part of the Rastafari culture and he really believed in it on a spiritual level. His herb was an extension of himself and not just a general commitment.

When I reflect on the images I took of Peter, I am left with the impression of him as an elitist. His posture, presence, and smile, the way he looked at the camera communicate to me that he was a strong, totally in-charge person. I admired the guy a lot and was impressed that he did the best he could with the limited opportunities he had been given.

Peter was a true artist and used his music and philosophy to get his art across. He was a really great entertainer who loved to perform. Peter was very talented and could play many different instruments – keyboards, hand drums, the piano, etc. The only instrument that I never saw him play was the bass. Peter did not do bubblegum music; his music was tight and always had a message. He knew how to talk and use language as a device to get his message out. He understood the power of words and music as a universal language, was optimistic that the world could be a better place and that he was the one to spearhead this change.

Peter had a very good understanding of other genres of music and liked to listen to black jazz musicians like Herbie Hancock, but he really did not have a love for Rock and Roll music. Like most Jamaicans, he was partial to reggae music.

A mystical person, Peter was also very intellectual, but not so much school-wise. Additionally, he was charming and really loved kids. At clubs, whenever he saw someone with a baby, the first thing he would do was go over to them and try to hold their baby in his arms. Being on the road a lot, Peter did not have many opportunities to have such a normal and personal life, so when the opportunity came, he grabbed it and cherished it until the next one came along. His relationships with women were not casual; I admire the fact that when we were on tour, he was not promiscuous like some of his peers. He stayed committed to his partner in each subsequent relationship.

It was interesting to be a friend of his. Peter was fun to be with, and a lot of times, I'd simply put the camera in the bag and just listen to him. He liked to make fun of people who were too serious. Sometimes, he would pull his glasses down his nose like a professor and mimic – he loved to ridicule high society. While I never really discussed Peter's upbringing with him, I suspect that his having been subjected to the inequalities of the colonial plantation Jamaican culture greatly affected him.

Peter could be outrageous with his points of view on life. Interestingly enough, nobody really challenged his belief systems. I being more of a pragmatist just laughed and said, 'Ya mon!' most of the time. I recall Peter telling me on one occasion that Jamaica was prosperous and agricultural enough to feed the world. He was very entertaining. I never got tired of his company. He was bigger than life. He lived the life and was representative of it. On and off stage, he was not any different as a person. Peter was the real deal.

My Table Talks
with Tosh
by Roger Steffens

Peter's was a voice for the ages, important most especially to the struggling underclass internationally. In Africa, he is more revered even than Marley because of his unrelenting militancy.

What struck me most about him was his dreadly serious demeanour in public, but privately, he was a very warm and humourous person. You always laughed around him. Particularly inviting was Peter's deconstruction of the language as he referred to his manager as his damager, calling our town Follywood and city Hellay. He called the leader of Jamaica, 'The Crime Minister who shit in the House of Represent-a-T'ief.' He ripped apart the word friend to reveal that 'fri' means to bring heat upon and 'end' is elimination. 'So check it out,' he demanded, 'Who are your friends?' And it was, indeed, a so-called friend who killed him.

I first met Peter after his surprise appearance at Bob Marley's concert in the Burbank Starlight Amphitheater (Los Angeles) in the summer of 1978. Unknown to Bob, he had come to see the show and when Bob returned to the stage for his encore of 'Get Up, Stand Up,' which they had co-written, he burst out from the wings in the middle of it, just at the point where he comes in on the record, and took the microphone from Bob and began singing his part. Bob was ecstatic, jumping up and down with uncontained glee, a huge smile on his face.

Three years later, I interviewed Peter about that evening for my TV show and asked what went on after the Burbank event. He told me he had gone to Bob's dressing room and Bob clapped his hand and said, 'Bwoy, the Pope feel that one!'

Roger and Tosh at
Hank Holmes's Reggae Archives,
Los Angeles, California, 1979
©Roger Steffens/Roger Steffens's
Reggae Archives

Then, looking straight into the camera, Peter announced, 'And three days later the Pope died!'

On our first long talk in September of 1979, he recalled being stoned with money at the Ward Theatre when The Wailers appeared there in the mid-1960s. He filled both pockets of his pants, but by the time the show was over, the audience had begged it all back from him.

A different kind of conversation came in 1983, also captured on video, in which he spoke of the numerous plots on his life that he felt were being mounted against him. He also claimed that it was Chris Blackwell who first called the group Bob Marley and the Wailers, which is totally backwards. Even though I showed him records going back as far as The Wailers' debut, 'Simmer Down,' with 'Bob Marley and the Wailers' as the credit on the label, the entire output of Wail'N/Soul'M which credit most records on their own label to 'Bob Marley and the Wailing Wailers', and the Upsetter era which also credited 'Bob Marley and the Wailers,' he refused to back down. I was shocked by his inability to change even when confronted with facts.

As the two new deluxe repackagings of *Legalise It* and *Equal Rights* were issued recently, renewed attention is being paid to these significant landmarks in the history of reggae. *Legalise It*, for which I wrote the liner notes, contains the original, 'unoverdubbed' version of the album as well as a number of fine dub plates he made privately for various sound systems. There is little left in the vault now, but I hope that we shall discover more vital material to share with a new audience.

The **Gentle Giant**

by Doug Wendt

I feel very fortunate to have been able to watch Peter perform live on several occasions and also to have conducted an amazing interview with him. Peter was very brave and talented. He was relentlessly determined to speak the truth despite the repercussions. Once I got to know Peter well I discovered that beneath his often stern and militant demeanour, he was actually a very gentle giant. He was one of the sweetest people one could ever meet. I know by being tall myself that Peter was probably unaware of what he was projecting. He most likely did not view himself as an imposing figure that exudes authority.

One of the things that I really appreciated about him was the way he used words with a Rastafarian twist – he was a wordsmith unlike any other. He would turn words inside out and break them down, to make them more 'overstandable.' I would not be surprised if some of the words Peter coined last forever, even superseding some original words that don't make the same sense as his puns.

Some other qualities of his that have made a lasting impression on me are his militancy and political consciousness, coupled with his real sense of urgency about fixing the ills in society. He believed that the system was a fraud, the dollar would die, etc. In 1974 when I began doing my reggae radio show it was amazing to finally begin hearing all of Peter's works at once, both solo and with The Wailers, that he had been releasing since the early 1960s.

One of my favourite videos of him is of a press conference where he goes off against songs of personal love as being too dominant in the culture. I share Peter's sentiments on this matter. As far as he was concerned, we can have plenty of love songs after we have remedied our social flaws, but first, let's take care of business.

My exposure to Peter's music is a result of my living in San Francisco and attending the Art Institute where I studied filmmaking. In the fall of 1973, I heard that the Jamaican film, *The Harder They Come* (by the late Perry Henzell) was playing at the Surf Theatre, near the beach in San Francisco. My friends told me that I had to see it. I did and was so impressed that the next day I bought its soundtrack album.

A couple weeks later, there was a little filler-like notice placed in the *San Francisco Chronicle* announcing that a Jamaican band called The Wailers would be playing at the Matrix that night. I really loved Toots & the Maytals's music in Henzell's movie, because Toots revived the style of Otis Redding, who I miss a lot. I thought that since these musicians must also have been in *The Harder They Come,* this show was going to be really great! So, my wife and I decided to attend The Wailers' concert. There were approximately 100 to 150 other people in attendance, many of them artists and other so-called 'early adapter' visionary type of people, including the famous beatnik poet Lawrence Ferlinghetti.

...we can have plenty of love songs after we have remedied our flaws...

After the hippie folk singer who opened the show exited the stage, the curtains reopened and in front of us stood Bob Marley, Peter Tosh, Joe Higgs, the Barrett brothers, 'Wia' Lindo, and other band mates, all of whom, up until that moment, had been unknown to me. They proceeded to do the material almost exactly as it is heard on Bob Marley and The Wailer's *Talking Blues* album, which was recorded at the Sausalito Record Plant around that same time. Since they were not in Henzell's film, I had no expectations, or knowledge of them. I thought that if they are so talented, and were not even in *The*

Harder They Come, but were also from Jamaica, something major must be going on music-wise on that little island. Henzell's movie exposed the connection between the police, politics, and drugs. The Wailers similarly illustrated the intrinsic corruption of 'the system' in their compositions.

While I was growing up in Montana, there was a famous rock band from nearby Spokane called The Wailers who first did 'Louie Louie.' Seeing Bob Marley and The Wailers reminded me of their American namesake. I realised that their reggae music was basically picking up the gauntlet of the music from the late 1960s which by 1973 had pretty much disappeared in the US due to the corporate takeover of radio. The wonderful, revolutionary music of the late sixties renaissance about peace and love, with a hard-hitting message, was basically wiped clean from the commercial airwaves. By 1973, I was sick and tired of hearing rock 'n' roll's elongated ego-driven retreads of what I had once loved growing up. I was really hungry to hear some powerful and succinct music that continued progressive themes like the Motown songs done by Marvin Gaye, The Temptations, and others who did 'What's Going On,' 'Mercy Mercy Me (The Ecology),' 'Ball Of Confusion' and many more.

Witnessing Peter and the other Wailers' live performance at The Matrix made such a great impression on me that the very next day I walked down to Tower Records and purchased six or seven reggae albums including The Wailers' *Burnin'* and *Catch A Fire*, plus some of various artists' compilations on the Trojan Records label out of England. I soon packed almost all my rock 'n' roll albums into a trunk and put them in my attic.

From then on through the mid-eighties, I almost exclusively bought reggae music before expanding into World Beat. It was not until the late seventies that I discovered all the rare and amazing work that Peter had done solo and as one of The Wailers during the sixties. When I reflect on Peter as a solo artist, I consider him to be one of the best; he is up there with Bob Marley, Joe Higgs, Linton Kwesi Johnson, Mutabaruka, Bob Andy, Sister Carol and a few others. Looking at Peter from the perspective of all music history, I place him in the highest echelons with artists like John Lennon because of his ability to be so fearless and really tap into the truth while making it palatable, digestible, informative, and entertaining for the public.

Peter, who was professionally influenced by performers such as Curtis Mayfield and The Impressions, obviously felt that whatever was inside of him would be easier to express via his music. Personally, his work is significant to me because it continues the spirit of the sixties. He was a conduit for all the best aspects of this era – the absolute yearning of the world's youth for a much better world, one that is possible to achieve if we would just buckle down and pay attention to the things that need to be changed.

Peter's work was nurtured in Jamaica, a very mystical land of wood and water, and combined with the uniqueness of Ethiopia, and its African connection to Haile Selassie. Both countries were never really conquered totally. The Maroons in Jamaica also add another strain of rebelliousness to the hundreds of years of influences in the background of Peter's compositions.

It was like a shot of adrenaline the night I saw The Wailers perform at the Matrix. When the sixties came to an end with Altamont and the campus murders at Kent and Jackson State Universities in 1970, the consciousness of that period and the first half of the twentieth century were nearly destroyed. There was a concerted effort to dumb everything down. Black music was eliminated from some rock 'n' roll radio stations, as were any type of protest songs. With the advent of corporate mergers and the reactionary and religious right-wing's counterattack starting in the early seventies, Peter, Bob, and The Wailers arrived at just the right time with their much needed breath of fresh air.

I think of this moment as a personal epiphany, another instance of me being unexpectedly and happily blindsided.

The Wailers' music was so powerful, yet very different from the material in Henzell's film. It was incredible to hear, for the first time ever, 'Rastaman Chant,' 'Get Up, Stand Up,' 'Burnin' and Lootin,' '400 Years,' 'No Sympathy,' 'Slave Driver,' etc., in that little North Beach club. Their style of reggae was just phenomenal and on another level. To see them in this phase of their career when they were so fully developed and so ready to get discovered on an international level was absolutely amazing!

In addition to 'Get Up, Stand Up,' 'The Day the Dollar Die,' 'The Poor Man Feel It' and 'Fools Die,' the other songs by Peter that speak to me the most are his spiritual compositions such as 'Igzhiaber,' 'Rastafari Is,' and 'Creation,' which really touch me on a deep level.

In 1973 or 1974, Tony Wright, a.k.a. Tony Moses, and myself were the first west coast DJs to play reggae on the radio. Tony was the first person to expose me to dub music which I believe is the

The Wailers music was so powerful, yet different...

most influential style of reggae to emerge from Jamaica. That really sealed my total love for reggae. I play dub all the time on my Midnight Dread radio show. I also dug how Peter and his band used the dub technique while he gave his 'livatribes' or sang.

In August of 1983, I had the chance to interview Peter, thanks to his late publicist Charlie Comer, who represented artists such as the Beatles. He was very happy to do the same for Peter. Charlie was already familiar with me and my work which ensured that I had the opportunity to interview Peter when he was in San Francisco. One day, Charlie called to inform me that Peter was staying at the Golden Gateway Inn, on Van Ness Avenue, which was just a couple of blocks from my apartment near Nob Hill in San Francisco, so we scheduled the session for August 17.

Late in the morning the day of the interview I walked with my tape recorder down the street two blocks to meet Peter. When I entered his hotel room, the first thing that caught my eye was the huge wad of money that he had on his night table. It was from the proceeds of a concert he had played the night before, which had gone really well. Once I had set up my tape deck and microphones I started the interview. After my first question, Peter jumped up and grabbed his little mini-cassette recorder and stated, 'I want to record this, I don't usually get to do interviews like this.'

I guess he was really impressed with my first question, which I prefaced with,

...how horrible the promotion of reggae music had been in the States.

You've been involved with several labels in America – Columbia, Rolling Stone, EMI – and I must tell you in ten years of playing strictly reggae music on commercial radio I have never received one promotional copy of any of your records. That means they're not taking care of business, they're not dealing with even commercial radio.

Our interview was intense and Peter got really fired up because I told him the truth about how horrible the promotion of reggae music had been in the States. For quite some time, I had been the only reggae show on commercial radio. Still, major labels would never send me reggae promos; it was as if I did not exist. I would have to go to a secondhand music store and purchase a copy of Peter's and other reggae artists' work if I wanted to play their music on the air.

I had been on an FM station on Sunday nights during the period that there was still a lot of public service consciousness in my country, and Sunday nights nationwide was when the radio stations would do a lot of public service shows as was required by law. When I worked the 10 o'clock to 2 o'clock, or the 10 o'clock to 1 o'clock shift, I was one of the few music shows on the air; everything else was talk, or public service programmes. So, folks searching the dial would only find my show to listen to often if they wanted to hear music. That made it possible for me to reach a lot of people and introduce them to reggae.

I was very blessed to have interviewed Peter and considered our session about the best interview I have ever done. Peter said things to me which he had not previously mentioned in other interviews. I was thrilled that I had recorded our exchange and I could later transcribe to publish it in *Beat* magazine, plus use it on my radio shows. Upon arriving back home, I played the tape. When I asked Peter, 'Did The Wailers engage in original science?' the tape went dead. This scared me because it was a question about mysticism. Thinking maybe my playback machine was faulty, I decided to play the cassette in another recorder. When that did not work I tried to play it in my car, and again later, at a friend's house. There was nothing on almost the whole tape. I was so upset that I wrote a cryptic symbol on the casing which only I would recognise and threw it in a box with a bunch of junk tapes in my attic. It was really heartbreaking for me!

On Friday night September 11, 1987, I received a phone call from Roger Steffens in Los Angeles informing me of the awful report that Peter had been shot dead. This was just the worst news possible. At that time, I was employed by KFOG, the major classic rock station in San Francisco, a highly successful commercial station even to this day. I did an hour of Midnight Dread reggae shows there during prime time Tuesday nights, which was cool since a lot more people could hear the programme. I had top ratings and the show was always sold out with sponsors to the point that people who wanted to could not buy ads.

I remembered that when John Lennon was murdered most of the radio stations in San Francisco began playing his music nonstop. They played his controversial songs like 'Woman is the Nigger of the World,' and other hard-core truths and rights Lennon tunes. Some were very powerful and maybe even politically incorrect, so they have not been heard on the radio since – except maybe for public radio. In the immediate aftermath of Lennon's death, radio hosts had a brief licence to let it all out. Since the station manager, advertiser, or the audience would not likely register any complaint about anything that I might do on my Tosh Tribute show, I had the opportunity to cover Peter in any way that I felt appropriate. In the emotion of the moment I believed that anything from our interview was fair to consider for commercial radio play.

Since I had a few days to prepare a proper memorial programme dedicated to Peter's life and music, I remembered the tape of the interview I had conducted with him four years earlier and the fact that the first part of the interview was audible. While some people may be skeptical about my narrative, I would encourage them to check out all my shows from the period when I interviewed Peter through the time leading up to his death and they will discover that at no time did I ever play anything from that session on any of my shows. This was because most of the interview, as far as I was concerned, did not exist. It had somehow been erased, or poorly recorded, or there was a technical problem, or maybe even some supernatural force at work.

I decided to go up to the attic to look for the tape. It was not easy to find as it was covered with dust. I wiped it off and put it in the cassette player. To my utter surprise, the entire interview was there. It was kind of frightening! I felt as if I had tapped into something very deep and it could only be exposed properly after Peter's death. While I was crushed by his murder, I was also ecstatic that I could now spread Peter's message on my show and in *Beat* magazine. Later, I also posted it in its entirety on my *midnightdread.com* website.

A few years later, while working as a projectionist in movie theatres, I was at the Roxy Theatre in San Francisco to see the premiere of *Red X*. For the first showing I did not have to project, so I watched the film with the audience. As I viewed the movie,

I was surprised to hear my voice intermittently throughout the documentary. It then dawned on me that a lot of the movie featured my interview with Peter. Wayne Jobson, the Co-Executive Producer of the film, and Peter's domestic partner, Marlene Brown, had found the mini-cassette of the recording that Peter had made of our interview (which incidentally, he had also played for EMI Records the week following our meeting).

When I reflect on Peter's legacy, I expect three things: 1. He will become as well-known and as appreciated as Bob Marley, and they and other reggae artists will gain wider acceptance in the music industry. It was not until Bob's death that Bob became really popular in the US and that is probably because he was now viewed as being less of a threat to society. 2. People will take Peter's message seriously and act on it. All of the ideas which he expressed in his music need to be made a priority and seen as the first order of business. The bottom line is that *...we must be willing to 'Get up, Stand up'* we must be willing to 'Get up, Stand up.' There was a movement in which people planned to show up en masse in Washington, DC to effect social and political change. If we are going to have one heart, one aim, one destiny, we definitely will have to come together. We cannot continue to blame the poor for our problems. It is obvious that the Establishment is not going to initiate this required change, since the cause of humanity's decline is that the Babylon system is a fraud. So, I am looking forward to seeing if this rally will be the spark to spearhead change, or if we are going to have to wait even longer. 3. Tosh's legacy will continue to mushroom and he will be seen as an amazing prophet who exposed hard truths. Despite the current superficiality of dancehall music, Peter's nutrient-rich, revolutionary message will rise and outlast it.

A Most
Unique Artist

by Dick Wingate

There was never a dull moment with Peter Tosh, one of the most unique artists of the 1970s and 1980s. Although Peter was not the most talented musician or singer that I ever worked with, he was unquestionably one of the most passionate and definitely the most political. Also, he was 'of the people,' not above the people. He never adopted a lifestyle of a big star.

Peter was a lightning rod for the music, politics, and culture of the Third World, and his charisma and delivery made up for any shortcomings he had musically. His approach to music and writing was inexorably tied up into the message he was delivering. It is impossible to separate them. Peter would take simple ideas and turn them into rhythmic calls to action. The listener couldn't resist either the music track, or the message. Additionally, Peter could be softer and more personal when he wanted to, on songs like 'I Am That I Am,' which, in my opinion, is one of his best crafted songs.

While employed at Columbia Records as his product manager, although I did visit Peter during the recording of *Equal Rights* in Miami, my involvement with this most unique artist revolved around the packaging, marketing, and promotion of his albums – which was no easy feat. I recall how challenging it was to get CBS (the owner of Columbia Records at the time) to issue the cover photo of *Legalise It*, and even more so, to get the company to agree to make 'Legalise It' rolling papers, which we distributed promotionally. Ultimately, we were happy with the success of the first album in establishing Peter as a solo artist, and were thrilled when his second album was even better.

In terms of my interactions with Peter, a favourite memory entails a funny story that illustrates his love of marijuana. I had to pick up Peter at the crack of dawn one morning at a New York hotel to bring him to WNEW-FM for an early radio interview with Dave Herman, their morning DJ. The station had been playing the first album and was very supportive. It was difficult to get Peter up. I had to go into his suite where his whole travelling entourage was basically still asleep. On the way to the station I told him that the station had only one rule for the visit and the interview: no smoking weed. WNEW-FM was owned by a big conglomerate, Metromedia, and I had been told by Dave Herman that they wouldn't tolerate any ganja being smoked anywhere on the premises.

We started the interview, but during the commercial break Peter decided to light up a spliff. Well, that was the end of the interview as you might imagine. There was just no stopping Peter! He needed ganja in the early morning like most people need coffee!

Peter's music had a universal message and his lyrics reflected the international political unrest of the time. Perhaps, his waning popularity is simply due to the passage of time. Overtime, Bob Marley's name has become synonymous with reggae, and I think Chris Blackwell, who founded and ran Island Records, had a lot to do with that. Furthermore, Marley's death was treated by the media as a much bigger event than Peter's. Also, one must take into consideration that Marley's catalogue is much more actively marketed and sold than Peter's. It is only now after all these years that Peter's first two solo albums are being given the proper reissues that they long deserved.

When I reflect on my last conversation with Peter, I am saddened by that memory. It was during the late 1980s and by now I had become head of A&R for PolyGram Records. Peter had been dropped by his third label, EMI and was out of a recording contract. One day, he called me at my office in New York from Jamaica and said he was working on new material and asked if I would like to listen to it. I was delighted to hear

from him as I had not spoken to him directly in many years, and of course, I wanted to hear the material. Sadly, before he could make it to New York, or send it to me, he was murdered. It broke my heart, but I am glad I had the chance to reconnect with him before he died. To this day, I still think about that conversation.

Left to Right: Dick Wingate of Columbia Records, Donald Kinsey of Word, Sound and Power Band, Peter Tosh and Ron McCarrell of Columbia Records at Chela Bay Hotel, Ocho Rios, Jamaica, 1976

*Performing with Kinsey in Augsburg, Germany
June 19, 1983
© Wolfgang Guerster
http://www.rock-shot.com/about_me.htm*

His
Brother's Keeper

by Donald Kinsey

One thing that I really loved about Peter was that he walked what he talked. Whenever Peter spoke, he said something deep! He had a way with words, and with other ways of expressing himself. He was and is still the Steppin' Razor.

Peter and I were very close, and would have some deep conversations. On one occasion, when we were talking he showed me a book about prophets, Selassie I and the powers of the spirit. It was really profound and I told Peter that when I was a kid, I would have out of body experiences. As soon as I said that to him, he replied, 'Yes, mon. That's something that Jah gives us, but we don't exercise it enough to its full potential.' It made me feel so good to know that Peter understood what I was talking about.

When I think about Peter, I think about my grandfather who my brothers and I used to visit in Mississippi in the 1960s. Back then, with all the racial tension that existed, it was not a good scene. There was an ongoing struggle, and the music, both blues and reggae, reflected this strife. Additionally, it gave people an outlet to express themselves. When I was first exposed to reggae, it immediately reminded me of the gospel music which I grew up playing in my grandfather's church. I could both hear and feel the truth and the struggle.

When I initially met Peter, I had a band by the name of White Lightning. My manager at the time was in touch with Lee Jaffe, who was then working with Peter. They made arrangements for me to meet Peter in New York, and when we met, we instantly clicked and decided to do some studio work together on the *Legalise It* album. After completing that project, Peter invited me to tour with him and I accepted his invitation.

Fusing my blues roots of playing with Peter's style was a natural thing because the blues is true music, coming up out of the cotton fields of Mississippi and the slave ships. It is real – a reality check. Blues, gospel and reggae music all go hand in hand. The kind of reggae music that Peter played was truth and justice. When I first heard it, I felt it and immediately wanted to play it.

Collaborating with Peter on the recording of the *Mama Africa* album evoked a very spiritual and magical feeling. The way the music came together was really a blessing. It was a very important time in music, in Peter's career, and in the scheme of world events. During that era something special was happening and I am just thankful that the band was able to record in that toxic period. Peter was given a mission and he was aware of it. He had insight and did what he was placed on this earth to do. There were a lot of factors that conspired to stop this tour from materialising, but it eventually happened. I am just grateful that we were able to take the music to the people on tour. It was like connecting all the pieces together for that album.

...had insight and did what he was placed on this earth to do.

For me, the best part of that tour was our stop in Swaziland. Our concert there was extremely special. It was like food for the soul! It was nourishment for all the spectators. I had never before seen so many African people in my life – it was cool! That was actually my first trip to Africa and apartheid was still going on in South Africa. Our accommodations were out in the bushes and I can remember rebels coming out of the bush and Peter giving them hats and t-shirts that were printed with the words, 'Mama Africa.' When I saw them coming out with their guns, all fighting in the name of the ongoing struggle in South Africa, I could identify with them. It was similar to the fight against slavery and racial segregation in America. Thank God, apartheid has been abolished! I like to feel that when we made this album, we helped to play a role in toppling and dismantling that system.

While on the Los Angeles leg of this tour, Peter was gifted with the M16 Stratocaster by an unidentified fan. This was a very unique moment. When the guy presented it to Peter, he was shocked. Although Peter had received many gifts before from fans, this present was very special to him. He could not believe that the brother had made it for him. The guitar was well put together. The stock looked almost like that of a real M16 weapon. I believe that the fan had actually made it with some parts from an M16 rifle. Peter was really pleased with the gift and said, 'Yes, mon! Now, I can kill the pirates!' He connected with the Stratocaster as soon as it was placed in his hands. He really loved to play this guitar and his face would light up when he used it.

Whenever he picked up this instrument it became more than just a guitar. Many guitarists call their guitars an axe. This Stratocaster was definitely Peter's axe. He used it to chop down a lot of inequities in the world. The fan that made the guitar for Peter could not have made it for a better man! He definitely understood Peter and what he was about. This instrument was indeed Peter's M16. He fought injustice with his music. Music was his weapon. It was his bullets. He would usually play the instrument twice during a show, and always when he was performing his song, 'Coming in Hot.' When he played that guitar, he was definitely making a statement at that particular time, during a show. He would shoot you down with his music. He would shoot you down with his lyrics.

I was honoured to play with Peter because I understood his mission. He was on a special assignment that only he could deliver. I realised it from the very first time that I met him. It was very spiritual and Peter was almost Christ like. Similar to Christ, he had to overcome a lot of things like being brutalised and scorned by people, but he kept on going. Peter was prophetic, knew the future, and even about his own death. He knew all that was to come. I feel blessed to have been one of his soldiers to help him with his mission. He had some of the greatest musicians around him – Santa Davis, Fully Fullwood, Keith Sterling, Steve Golding, Robbie Lyn. It was not easy bringing that music forward to the people, but through the blessings of the Almighty, this music could not be stopped. It is hard to think about all the things that Peter had to endure, but he was very strong and his music will live on.

On Jamming
With Peter – Part 1

by Robbie Shakespeare

Some music makers choose music, whereas music favours a few musicians. Peter was one of those artists who were called to the profession, similar to Sly Dunbar and me. When we initially started playing together, coming from Jamaica, there was not any real money in it for us. We entered our career because of our deep passion for music and our ability to use it to spread our message of love, political consciousness, and reggae. Despite the fact that Jimmy Cliff and Bob Marley were already spreading the word, many people were unaware of the various styles of reggae music that exist. Toots and the Maytals, Burning Spear, Peter Tosh, Black Uhuru, Sly and Robbie – we all play reggae, but our styles are very different and have a different feel.

Peter was very close to Sly and me and we would get together during the day at each other's home. We had great vibes and used to tease each other a lot. In Jamaica we call this jesting 'draw card.'

I first met Peter through Lee Jaffe, who one day asked me if I would be interested in playing with Peter Tosh, to which I replied, 'Yes.' At that time, I had the option of playing with Burning Spear, or to continue doing recordings. After I agreed to play with Peter, I assembled his original Word, Sound and Power band. Upon completing the *Legalise It* album, the decision was made for us to go on tour, so I started recruiting musicians such as Sly, Earl 'Wia' Lindo, Al Anderson, and a keyboardist whom we called 'Tarzan.' Subsequent tours over the years resulted in other musicians such as Mikey Chung, Keith Sterling, and Robbie Lyn joining the band.

Professionally speaking, there was great synergy among us that made our band a success. We worked well together as a team and Peter had a lot of confidence in my ability to complete his music for him. Sometimes he would start a song in the studio and I would finish it for him. That being said, although Sly and I would take charge, Peter was still the boss and respect is due.

I had a very positive experience jamming with Peter. While we did not have a set time each week for our band rehearsals, whenever it was close to the time for us to go on tours, we would get together, rehearse, and incorporate several songs in our programme. These tours are all significant to me as the Peter Tosh era opened 'Sly and Robbie,' to the audience we currently have, and it was a stepping stone for us to be seen visually. Concert-goers could now put our faces with our names. During live performances, after doing one or two encores, there were no more songs left for us to play, so Sly and I would just start dubbing. We developed the technique in which Peter would sing for awhile then stop. Next, Sly and I would dub for a bit, or just dub by ourselves at the end of the show. This led to people becoming exposed to and familiar with our dub style.

All the venues that we played, whether large or small, are memorable to me. However, the most memorable show I played with the Word, Sound and Power band was the first one with the Rolling Stones, in Philadelphia. This was also our first time performing for such a large crowd. Reflecting on these performances, while I cannot single out a particular song of Peter's that I enjoyed playing the most, I must say that all of his songs speak to and have a special meaning for me.

Considering my friendship with Peter offstage, I greatly benefitted from his sociopolitical wisdom. He, and also Herbie Miller for that matter, were very instrumental in my sociopolitical enlightenment and development. Both of them taught me a lot about important issues affecting the African Diaspora, such as, Nelson Mandela's struggles and the system of apartheid. Since they were more politically aware than me, I had many questions for them and their answers opened my eyes to certain things occurring around the globe.

In addition to Peter's valuable socio-political lessons, in general, I have always appreciated his astuteness and wit. Similar to my father, he told me many things that have stayed with me over the years. Even when Peter was not directing his comments at me, I can still remember things that he said because they were so insightful and funny. I recall on one occasion when he was being interviewed, during the time when the drug LSD was very popular, the interviewer remarked, 'Peter! What do you think about LSD?' Peter without missing a beat replied, 'Lucifer the Son of Death.' That quote of Peter's ended up being circulated in many US magazines for quite some time, as the quote of the week.

Due to our closeness, I would accompany Peter on his interviews to ensure that he did not go overboard with his comments since we were coming from Jamaica and reggae then was not readily accepted by mainstream listening and viewing audiences. He could become very emotional and start saying things that I felt people would view as too radical, scaring them away. So, I went along with him to ensure that he remained calm and shared his views gently.

Looking back on my association with Peter, as my friend and former music partner, most of all I miss his physical and musical presence. Someone like Peter comes along probably every 100 or 1,000 years. He was unique, unafraid to speak his mind, and cleverly set his opinions to music that everyone can enjoy. A brilliant guitarist, keyboardist, and harmonica player, I have never met someone else who could come up with words as fast as Peter. His contribution to music is just as valid as that of artists who went before and came after him. He is no longer here with us, so we will never get his special kind of music any more.

Sly, Peter and Robbie at the Olympia Hotel in front of the College of Arts, Science and Technology (CAST), Jamaica, April 23, 1978
© Avrom Robin/Susan Finkelstein

On Jamming
With Peter – Part 2

by Lowell 'Sly' Dunbar

I have a lot of respect for Peter and feel really blessed that he allowed me to become a member of his band. Having grown up listening to The Wailers, which was the group that inspired many Jamaican artists, and then being able to play with one third of The Wailers was a great experience for me. Robbie was the one who asked me to join Peter's band. He and I used to do a lot of sessions together, so I accepted his invitation. I have never forgotten that moment when Robbie took me to meet Peter, or regretted my decision to join his Word, Sound and Power band.

When Robbie introduced me to Peter, he said, 'This is Sly the drummer,' and Peter responded, 'Alright.' Back then, I played a different style and he said, 'I want One Drop.' I replied, 'No problem.' At that time, the 'Rockers' style that I played was popular both in Jamaica and around the globe, and people were yearning for it. It took me a little while to sneak it in on Peter and he did not even say anything. He realised that we had to move forward with the music. He understood that was my way of expressing on the drums what he was singing.

Peter was the one who really launched 'Sly and Robbie' as a unit on stage, so people could really see what we did inside the studio live on stage, and I thank him very much for that. This was the time when Robbie and I started shaping ourselves into the perfect unit.

The thing that I admired most about working with Peter was his giving us the freedom to play as we saw fit. He never once dictated to us how we should perform. At nighttime, Robbie and I used to sit in a room and discuss ways that we could improve our performance from the previous night by doing different things.

Prior to going on stage, Robbie and I would spar like boxers in an arena. We would work up a sweat to get our adrenaline flowing, and I would also pray for a good show. In contrast, Peter was always very calm and just went on stage in a positive mood. He knew that he had a good band behind him, and that we were there to support him 100 per cent. Furthermore, Peter was aware that if anything went wrong, we would cover it up, so the audience would not even be aware that something was off. Peter loved performing, and sometimes Robbie would go over to him and say, 'Dance man, dance!' Then, Peter would put down his guitar and start jumping around.

In terms of arranging the show, Peter left everything up to us. For a man of his status in reggae, one would expect him to want to call the songs as he pleased, but he never did so at any time when I was a member of his band. He always left that task up to *Peter's music is one of a kind; it has a distinct sound.* Robbie and me. We would select the list and he would say to us, 'Jus' call the tune dem Papa. Jus' call the tune.' Since he did not have to be concerned about which song should be played next, he could concentrate on playing his guitar.

There was a musical magic to Peter's songs and the rhythm grooves that were set to them. We always looked to Africa for that rhythm section and then would convert that sound into a reggae beat and attempt to do a mixer. People find music therapeutic, so we always tried to make it soothing for them by implementing little things such as percussions that they would find nice.

While there were no special traditions that Peter had for the band to celebrate a successful show, after each performance he would say, 'Yes, Papa, we give it to them!' In our hearts, we thought every concert was great because we put our all into our performances. We did not care about the critics' reviews;

we just played for our audience and gave them what they wanted, night after night.

This was also the case when we played with Peter at the Montreux Jazz Festival in 1979, which I recall as being a good show. We did not concern ourselves with what the other bands were doing. We just did what we came to do and performed to the best of our ability.

In 1981, Robbie and I had the opportunity to work with Grace Jones in Nassau on 'Pull Up to the Bumper,' and also the late Gwen Guthrie on her album. That led us to try to get Peter to do some of that stuff, but he was not interested in their style of music. This was fine, but Robbie and I wanted to branch out after producing Black Uhuru, and so, despite the fact that Peter was at the height of his career, we made the decision to quit Word, Sound and Power.

Robbie and I left Peter in 1981 to tour with Black Uhuru. When we departed, we took with us some of the elements we had learned from him, however, Black Uhuru had a different sound. We tried to fuse theirs with Peter's, but it did not really work. There is a saying that 'Ska is the father and Rocksteady the son.' Sticking with that analogy, I would say that, Peter was the father and Black Uhuru the child because, while playing with them, Robbie and I were also shaping them.

Peter's music is one of a kind. It has a distinct sound. If you were to try to match the rhythm section on his songs 'Crystal Ball' and 'Don't Look Back' with that of other artists, you wouldn't be successful. The closest you would come to finding an equivalent is with the music of Black Uhuru, and that is because we were producing that group while collaborating with Peter.

Today, when I listen to Peter's songs, I really feel them and realise now their greatness. While playing with his band, I did not have such an understanding because of being caught up in the scene. Now that I am no longer involved with it, I can understand better the whole concept of Peter's music. His music is totally different from that of other artists and what is being produced in the recording studio today. If you listen to Peter's version of 'Steppin' Razor,' 'Get Up, Stand Up!' 'Recruiting Soldiers,' or his duet with Gwen Guthrie entitled, 'Nothing But Love,' and listen to how he is singing, you will see that he is in a league of his own. His song, 'Nothing But Love,' is still wicked! I played it quite recently for somebody and the person almost cried. The rhythm groove and how Peter and Gwen sang on that song is just fantastic!

I credit Peter's freestyle for helping Robbie and me to excel in our music careers. I recall that when we were doing 'Buk-In-Hamm Palace,' Robbie and I just started a groove while Peter strummed his guitar. Then he began to sing, 'Light up yu spliff, Light up yu chalice.' I turned to him and said, 'That wicked yu know,' and he laughed and said, 'Yes, Papa!' Then he started grooving, and we just had a good time with it.

When reviewing Peter's work, one can see that he was very much ahead of his time. Take for instance the system of apartheid. Peter was quite knowledgeable about it before most of us. The first time that I heard the word 'Apartheid,' I thought that Peter had coined it because he was very good at making up words. He was so on it back then, and was the only artist chanting about the evils of apartheid without caring about the consequences of his actions.

For such an accomplished artist to receive no airplay – not even in his homeland – is unfortunate. Radio stations should be more open to playing Peter's music, so that people can become familiar with it and have the freedom to decide if they like it or not. I hope that sooner rather than later, this will come to pass.

In Jamaica, I would love to see Peter's music being re-released and distributed, so people can purchase his work conveniently. There are still local people who appreciate his music and would love to be able to access it in music shops across the island.

I would like people to reflect on the strong messages in Peter's songs and come to understand what he was talking about. If they look at the condition of the world today, the problems in the Middle East, etc., they will see that Peter had prophesied these very same events.

Maybe Peter is going to be the stone that the builder refuses, but my hope for his legacy is that future generations will come to accept and love his music. Peter's music is real and it needs to be preserved, so others can enjoy and learn from it.

Sly, Avrom Robin, Peter and Robbie at the Olympia Hotel in front of the College of Arts, Science and Technology (CAST), Jamaica, April 23, 1978

Bittersweet
Memories
by George 'Fully' Fullwood

I am not going to tell you that Peter was perfect, he was not. None of us human beings are perfect, we all make mistakes. But musically speaking, he was a great and fun artist. Peter was a very sincere man who tried to rectify the injustices in this world. It deeply saddens me that his work, which was just as great as Bob Marley's, does not get much attention today.

If you did not really know Peter, he may come across as gruff, but in actuality, he was a gentle person. Due to this negative impression of Peter, sometimes people were reluctant to approach him. However, once they struck up a conversation with him, they came to realise that he was very interesting.

I have many wonderful memories of Peter. Some of them are of our travels on the bus. We would talk and laugh a lot and he would share a lot of stories with me – especially about ghosts and vampires. Peter was a very funny guy, and would always tell jokes. Many people did not know that Peter was such a fun person to be with.

Another strong recollection is of the occasion when Peter was doing a show and a white female journalist wanted to talk with him, but she was afraid to approach him. I saw her and enquired if she wanted to speak with Peter and she informed me that she did, but she had heard that Peter did not like white people. Therefore, I told her to come with me and took her to meet him. I used to call Peter 'Bush' and said to him, 'Bush, this lady want to talk to you man.' He replied, 'Yeah mon! Come talk to me.' After she had spoken with Peter, she approached me and said, 'Thank you so much. Oh gosh, it was so great! I am so happy I got to meet him!' I asked her if she was still afraid of Peter and she said, 'Oh no, I better understand him now.' So, I replied, 'You see, you should not judge anybody before speaking with them.' She then told me that she had just learned a lesson.

I also have fond memories of touring with Peter in Africa in 1983. I recall that on one occasion when we were doing sold out shows in Swaziland, thousands of Africans wanted to attend, but they could not gain admission. Peter stopped the performance and said to the promoter, 'I will not sing another note unless you let all of my brothers and sisters come in.'

Peter was well-loved in Africa. He had written a song called 'Mama Africa,' and every time he would sing it, the Africans would jump up and down with joy. I think that if Peter was still alive and decided to run for office in Africa, he would be quickly elected. Although Peter loved Africa, he was, however, concerned about the numerous tribal divisions that created discord amongst the Africans.

All my interactions with Peter told me who he was as a person. My history with Peter dates back to the time when he was one of the original Wailers before they became so popular. I used to both record and play with them at different clubs across Jamaica when I was with my band, the Soul Syndicate and Lee 'Scratch' Perry was producing us on the Upsetter label. Later, I had the opportunity to work with Peter as a solo artist after Sly and Robbie moved on.

As a bass player, I am a very creative person and my head is always full of ideas. Words cannot fully explain the collaborative process of making music with Peter because he was the kind of man who loved anything his musicians played and he never complained. I thought this was a good thing too because it demonstrated Peter's faith in us and was very telling of his character in choosing to work with us. While a member of Word, Sound and Power band, I had a lot of fun just creating stuff. It was a really great time for exploring the process of producing music.

Peter was one of the greatest and the best band leader I have ever worked with in my life. He had this mystique about him that people found very fascinating. On stage, you could sense his power and self-confidence. When we were performing, Peter never looked back at us in any negative way. He was always smiling and confident about our abilities. Similar to the other guys in the band, when on stage, I just let myself go because Peter was very receptive to our playing and believed in us. He would say 'Yesss!' This made working with Peter a lot of fun. Backstage after the show Peter would always say, 'Yeah mon! Wicked show! We kill dem mon!' His comments made us feel good.

Except for his struggles with the Jamaican authorities over the use of ganja, I believe that Peter was really loved by his fellow citizens. People who knew Peter and understood his work all loved him. There is an expression, 'A king is not a king in his own country until he goes out and conquers.' So, while Jamaicans loved Peter, he was not fully accepted by them until he had made a name for himself internationally like Bob Marley had done.

Although his memory is fading in certain parts of the world, I believe that it will always be here. Peter's words were very influential, truthful, and reflected what was happening in society. I was blessed to have been able to travel with Peter all over the world from 1981 right up until the time of his death.

The week before his death, he had called me from New York. Peter informed me that he and EMI had settled out of court for a lot of money. He said to me, 'Wh'appen man, you alright? You want me send you some money?' I said, 'Alright man, if you feel like it.' Peter then sent me a couple thousand dollars. He was a very generous individual.

Peter's posthumous win of a Grammy for *No Nuclear War* was bittersweet for me. It gave me a feeling of both happiness and confusion. Here it is, Peter, this great entertainer, who should have been here, had won a Grammy, but he was not around to enjoy the honour. I wanted Peter to be there to accept the award himself and be able to celebrate his win with him, but he was not even aware of it. I have pictures of Peter in my studio. Every day I look at them. In one of them, he is riding his unicycle.

When his life was cut short, we were all set to go on a three or six month tour for *No Nuclear War*. In my opinion, Peter was going to be *massive*. I still have the itinerary of places where we played with Peter. Every one of his shows was sold out! I remember shows at venues like the Ritz club in New York and the Roxy Theatre in Los Angeles. His headliners at such establishments illustrate how powerful he was going to be. Unfortunately, this sad event happened. So, I feel compelled to keep his memory alive.

After Peter's death, I decided to do my part by going on the road with my own band to places such as Brazil and Europe to play his songs. It was very tough because of the out-of-pocket expenses we incurred from staging these shows around the world, and the fact that today's concert-goers are more interested in other styles of music, but I am very proud of my efforts because Peter never got the opportunity to fulfil his mission. I had a lot of respect for Peter and I know that he also respected me. As long as I am alive, I plan to keep Peter's memory going as best as I can.

On 'Bush'
the Mystic Man

by Dennis Thompson

When I think of Peter Tosh, the words 'Mystic Man' come to mind because he was always fascinated by mysticism, believed that the mind is endless, and that we have the ability to think more than we actually do. He felt that for us to be able to just levitate was a great thing. Due to his belief in the great healing value of all plants, whether for medicinal or other purposes, I thought that 'Bush' was the perfect nickname for him, and so I used to call him by that moniker.

I initially met Bush when he was one of The Wailers. Similar to many Jamaicans, I regarded Bob Marley, Peter Tosh, and Bunny Wailer as Jamaica's version of the English rock band, the Beatles. Whenever The Wailers recorded in the studio, the Jamaican government paid close attention because they knew that they were an influential group and the people listened intently to what The Wailers said.

I recollect that The Wailers would come to Randy's studio where I used to work with the late Errol Thompson. When they stopped by, it was a standing joke that they were going to tour. In jest I would say to them, 'You're not going on tour; you are going to the country to play at clubs in the bush.' From that banter, we developed a comfortable and natural rapport and a mutual respect for each other. In addition to being good-natured, they were also very genuine people.

Shortly thereafter, Bob invited me to tour with him as his engineer and I did so until his death. After his demise, Peter approached me and said, 'I need some help! I need you to come and fix some sounds for me.' So, I went with him to look at his equipment. After a close inspection of his apparatus, I condemned everything. I told him that there was nothing that he possessed that was any good and he asked me to build him a set. I agreed to assist him. He gave me the necessary money to purchase some quality equipment, and we started working together.

As our relationship evolved, I also got to know Bush on a personal level. One of the things that we had in common socially was our appreciation of spicy food. Bush not only enjoyed a good meal, but he was also quite adept at cooking. Actually, he was an excellent cook! I believe that his culinary skills were a result of his upbringing in Trench Town. He most likely learned how to cook from observing his relatives and the other tenants who also lived in his yard. It was not unusual for children growing up in those settings to see their grandmother, or mother preparing and cooking porridge and other dishes, so, it is only natural that those skills would rub off on Bush.

His specialty dish was fish. He really loved fish, especially the kind called Rockfish. This species of fish is huge and has a big head. He liked to use the fish head when cooking soup which we call 'fish tea' in Jamaica. Although we call it 'tea' do not let the name deceive you, it is not a light broth; Bush's fish tea was actually quite thick and hearty. It was like eating a complete meal. After eating a bowl of it, one would be full.

When Bush lived in New York, he would go to Chinatown to buy his fish, as fresh as possible, from the fish vendor because he did not like to buy the frozen ones at supermarkets. My first opportunity to sample his cooking arose one day when I had the occasion to take some tapes over to his apartment on Central Park West. He had just finished cooking and invited me to join him for some fish tea. He gave me this big bowl of stew. Being a pepper addict, I was in seventh heaven! With his scotch bonnet peppers, thyme and special brand of seasoning, Bush would make an excellent soup which had the texture of gel. If you like pepper, you would be fine with his cooking, but if you do not like hot food, you would be in trouble because he prepared his meals *very* spicy!

Sometimes when I would visit him, I would forget the number of the floor on which he resided. So, I devised the perfect solution for locating his apartment. Upon entering the elevator, I would press the buttons for all the floors. When the doors opened on each floor, I would sniff the air for the aroma of his fish. I would continue to do this until a whiff of fish hit me.

Since he was always mixing and blending spices, I think it fair to say that Bush was an adventurous cook. He liked to experiment with exotic dishes that he had discovered while on tour in Africa and other foreign lands. Upon returning home, he would test some of the condiments he had acquired abroad by combining them with his native Jamaican ingredients to use when cooking his fish.

Although Bush enjoyed putting a special twist on recipes, his culinary adventures were not restricted to his kitchen. He was also game for trying new dishes while dining out. I remember that he really loved to dine at a Korean restaurant on 72nd Street and we would frequently go there for kimchi, which is the national dish of Korea. Bush would go up the wall for a bowl of kimchi jjigae! He also liked to eat the Korean style fish and rice. I fondly recall that the staff at the restaurant knew Bush very well and always gave him the royal treatment.

...his culinary adventures were not restricted to his kitchen.

While Bush and I eventually developed a close personal bond, it was our careers that cemented our lifelong friendship. When I collaborated with him on *No Nuclear War,* I did not realise that would be his last album. Considering all that we went through to produce the album, I am very pleased, but actually amazed that it survived! I was in England doing an album with Steel Pulse when Bush called and told me about *No Nuclear War*. He said that he had finished recording it and wanted me to mix the music. I explained to him that I would be in England for another month, and he said that was alright, when I was done, I should come to Jamaica and visit him. After completing my project with Steel Pulse, and prior to going down to Jamaica to see Bush, I first flew to New York.

When I later arrived at his home in Jamaica, and we had time to catch up with each other, we settled down to business. I enquired, 'Where's the album?' He replied, 'The tapes are in the room.' I went into the room Bush had indicated, which was very dark, and saw the tapes stacked in a corner, in a pool of water. At that time, Bush was unaware that there was water on the floor. I picked up the first four tapes that were at the top of the pile to inspect them. When I reached the box containing the tapes on the floor, it was so soaked, that when I lifted it, the bottom gave way and the tapes fell out. I asked Bush what was on the tapes and he responded that was the title track. I replied, 'To "No Nuclear War"?' He affirmed, 'Yes, that's it!' We then purchased a case of hand towels and about a dozen bath towels and went to Music Mountain that same night to dry the tapes. This was a very tedious process because we could only dry an inch of tape at a time. A reel of those tapes, on average, run about 15 minutes in length at high speed, so at the rate we were able to move, it took us many hours to complete the task. First, we dried the tapes forward and then in reverse. It took us the entire night to finish this job. Later, Santa (Davis) came and overdubbed the drums and took the tapes with him to New York to finish the album.

In addition to the fact that this was the last project I had the opportunity to do with Bush, this album is meaningful to me because all the tracks are unique and they speak to me in different ways. It is for this reason that I cannot identify a specific song from the album as my favourite. I like all of them. All of the compositions have their own feel, sound, and identity.

While I regret that this was Bush's last album, I am glad that it was one of his best pieces of work and he ended on a high note. I was the engineer for the Grammys the night that Bush won for *No Nuclear War* in 1988. Although I am sorry that it was done posthumously, his being awarded a Grammy gave me a great feeling for several reasons. Firstly, it signified to me the industry's recognition and acceptance of him as an artist. Secondly, it was an indication of the increasing international appeal of reggae music in general. Lastly, it was nice to see one of the products that I had personally worked on being rewarded on that level.

I know that Bush would have loved being presented a Grammy! That award would have been significant to him because it would have led to many avenues and meant the opening up of career opportunities. From his conversation with me about *No Nuclear War,* I could tell that he felt that this album would be special. I recall him saying to me, 'I man, yu know seh dis is the biggest reggae album yu ever going to work on!' I replied, 'Really? I will play more albums than this,' but Bush insisted, 'Naw man! Dis one special!' For him, his albums were like reading the newspaper. He would read the news to learn what is happening in the world, then record music to reflect these pertinent issues. Although *Equal Rights* and *Legalise It* are excellent albums, I think that *No Nuclear War* really appealed to Bush because of what it entailed about the whole nuclear situation, pollution, etc.

Another project which he had been preoccupied with when he was assassinated, that showed great promise, was some autobiographical material. At the time of his death, he had been assembling a series of tapes which he called, 'Red X,' that reflected his ideas about life and things that he wanted to see done in the future. He had on occasion shared with me some of his plans for this project. Although these recordings were later used in a documentary about his life, since he was still in the process of working out his ideas, no one can really know what his intentions were for the outcome of these recordings. If Bush had been given the chance to complete them, I am sure that the way he intended to use them would have been markedly different to the manner in which they were utilised in the film.

When I reflect on Bush's prevailing image as a miserable and cantankerous person it annoys me because he was nothing like that in real life. He only reacted badly when provoked, or asked stupid questions. Unfortunately, the media would then take such incidents out of context and publish, or broadcast them, giving a bad impression of him. It is quite tragic that the press persists in portraying him in such a poor light. Contrary to popular belief, he was in fact, a very nice, genuine, and humble person. Having had the privilege of knowing both Bush and Bob well, I wish that they were still here. Given the benefit of hindsight, there is no doubt in my mind that today's music scene would be totally different if they were alive today.

Thompson, Tosh and Donald Kinsey producing a Ska band from Chicago during Tosh's last tour. In the rear from left to right: Kevin Smith, Jim Robinson & Kate Fagan of Heavy Manners at Chicago Recording Company.
© *Jim Pasta*

Peter Tosh
and Theology
by Reverend Canon Ernle P. Gordon

Peter was a mystic, and developed a Creation theology, which was reflected in his finest piece of reggae music, called 'Creation.' His theology made a link with the two worlds as he said,

> How old is the sun? Sun not temporary, not chronological. There is terracelestial and the celestial, I am here, there, and everywhere. I live among men, so I must adjust myself. When I go to the other planet, I must adjust myself there too, mon.*

He never left the vibrations of the spirit world and was always contacting this world in long hours of silence. Furthermore, he had a profound comprehension of the ancestors. How can we forget the reggae lyrics with regard to Moses and the Prophets?*

Psalm 27 is one of the finest manifestations of Hebrew Psalmody, which expresses the wonders of creation, and the symphony of divine intervention. It is theological poetry which motivates the mind to move towards the multisensory spirituality, where the human being comes to understand and to experience truth consciously. It is the type of truth that empowers but does not contaminate. It does not harm. It is in Tosh, whose philosophy dances with theology and is exposed to the aroma of subjective spirituality, where the medium (poetry, the lyrics and the music) is the message.*

He asserted that, 'Everybody wants to go to heaven, but nobody wants to die,' (very Hegelian). Hegel once remarked that, 'Music is a spiritualistic art, the art which can be thrilling truth, reproduce the innermost essence of the human soul, the infinite shades of feeling.' There is a connection between

Hegel's philosophy and Tosh's use of music and poetry. Although Hegel was not alive when Tosh was a superstar, some of his philosophical thoughts, were reflected in the way Tosh connected poetry and music. Poetry and music both employ sound, but in the service of the poet (like Tosh), it becomes articulate and a definite sound, a word, a language. Lyric poetry corresponds to music, which falls back upon the invisible world, called the human soul. Tosh reflects Hegel's intellectual thought, that is, there is an intimacy in thought between music and poetry, and the lyrics manifest the inner unconscious self, which is awakened to consciousness. Additionally, he was always searching for truth, and stated that, 'To have the truth in your possession you can be found guilty, sentenced to death.' This made him very critical of certain aspects of Colonial theology which we inherited.*

Tosh had knowledge of the plantation system and the planter class which reflected coercion, imposition and control. So, he alluded to this 'system' as the 'shitstem.'* He remarked,

> Our people have been divided for years under this shituational, religionistic, trickological realm, but it is through the generations that we have to be the observers, see what is going on to learn how to diagnose the symptoms to extract the disease and the germs from out of it, cause so much things going on in the world.

In this system, we become objects and not subjects. Peter must be understood as an integral part of the Caribbean theologians' struggle for a theology of exploration and transformation, in which the goal is to make the unconscious become conscious. Tosh reaffirmed that Caribbean theology is an integral part of the process known as the search for identity.* He was critical of the type of Biblical understanding, in which the black person was regarded as being born in sin and was shaped in iniquity, but, the Biblical text, affirmed that we were born very good and made in the image and likeness of God.

Peter Tosh, did not like the interpretation of some of our hymns which denigrated the human being – especially the black person.* An example of this is, 'Oh, precious is the flow, that makes me white as snow.' It is impossible for the blood of Jesus to make us whiter than snow. For Tosh, liberation from these Babylonian views entails radical doubting, questioning and investigating, which emancipates people from every easy manipulation, and from the mindless structures, created by people for the purpose of mystifying and exploiting others.

He helped to raise Caribbean theology to a new level of consciousness, where we began to explore the depths of Caribbean mosaic with a penetrative imagination, and perceptive vision. What Tosh is affirming is that we ought to own our ontological heritage, which involves how we define, interpret and write our own history.* We have to be very careful how we allow others to interpret our history. We are reminded that we ought to feel the passion of our historical revelation, which energises a new self meaning, a creative self-definition, especially among our African brothers and sisters in order to torpedo the ghost of the identity conflict and mis-definitions.

Our theology must give us a healthy view of ourselves, so it is very opportune that the Anglican Church which pioneered the first Reggae Mass, by the Right Reverend Alfred Reid, in 1974, decided to incorporate in the new Anglican Hymnal hymns from both Peter Tosh and Bob Marley.* Anglican Communion, which is a manifestation of the Incarnation, does not separate theology from the cultural context, matter from Spirit and the secular from the sacred. We must remember that the first five centuries of Christianity were dominated by black theologians from Africa. Caribbean religious experience must create human beings who are free to express themselves in the medium that reflects the Caribbean cultural mosaic, and so, reggae is the medium of the message.

The new hymnal for the Anglican Church in the province of the West Indies has incorporated not only a hymn done by Peter Tosh ('Creation,' based on Psalm 27, Anglican hymn 229) but from many Caribbean writers who manifest a dynamic spiritual force that is now present in the music of the region.**

These include the late Barry Chevannes and Noel Dexter. The Anglican Church in the Caribbean sought to 'Caribbeanise' the theology of the hymnal, and therefore, created a catechism which highlighted Creation theology rather than Fall-Redemption theology.

In order to understand Tosh's Creation theology, we should first define the difference between Creation theology and Fall-Redemption theology. Fall-Redemption theology is a creature that reflects a dualistic model and a patriarchal phenomenon. Its theology begins with sin and original sin, and generally ends with redemption. Fall-Redemption spirituality does not teach believers about the new creation or creativity; nor does it address the issues of justice, love for the earth, caring for the cosmos, social transformation and the God of joy and delight. In contrast, Tosh's theology reveals a Creation theology which is very spiritual and dynamic. His lyrics indicate that he was not an agent of Fall-Redemption but Creation theology. It is very clear that Tosh understood the theological implications of Genesis: 1, 26–27; and it is vital that we quote Genesis: 1, 26–27, in order to make the linkage between the Genesis Creation theology and the thinking of Tosh.**

The writer of Genesis wrote the following, 'Let us make humankind in our image, according to our likeness, and let them have dominion over the fish of the sea, and over the birds of the air, and over the cattle, and over the wild animals of the earth, and over ever creeping thing that creeps upon the earth. So God, created humankind in his image, in the image of God he created them, male and female he created them. God bless them.

Now, let us look at the depth of the verses of the 'Creation' song written by Peter Tosh:

1. Jah is my Health and my Strength.
2. Jah is my Shield upon my right hand and my left hand.
3. Jah is my Guide throughout this Creation.

4. Jah is my Guide when the Philistines came down upon me.
5. Jah is my Guide from the pestilence of darkness. **

His brand of theology seeks to open our creative thought process by a reflection on certain aspects with regard to healing in creation, which seeks to reflect restorative justice in the social order. Restorative justice is crucial for the healing of creation, as we become co-creators with God.

As the world is going through turmoil, Creation theology as depicted by Tosh has a tradition, and a past with historical and Biblical routes. It is through this Creation centred tradition that Tosh was able to offer a new paradigm for wisdom and human survival in this changing Caribbean ethos.

I am not suggesting that Tosh read the catechism of the Anglican Church, but it is obvious that the Anglicans in the Caribbean made the decision to function theologically with Creation theology rather than Fall-Redemption theology.**

*Excerpts from 'Peter Tosh – The Prophet of Consciousness and Conscience.' Presented by the Reverend Canon Ernle P. Gordon at the University of the West Indies, Mona (October 16, 2007).

**Excerpts from 'The Theological Context of Creation Theology and Peter Tosh.' Presented by the Reverend Canon Ernle P. Gordon (September 2011).

*Wearing a crown made by Mary Steffens with the lyrics to
'Legalise It,' Los Angeles, 1979
©Roger Steffens/Roger Steffens's Reggae Archives*

Epilogue

While it is not my place to try and reconcile Tosh's diametrically opposed persona with his anima, I think that a few statements about lessons I have learned from this project are in order. From my conversations with his associates, I gather that the spectre of controversy that continues to haunt him in death while understandable is not wholly justified. Yes, his manner of expressing himself at times with vituperations was off-putting. Yes, his being principled to a fault may have cost him many wonderful career opportunities. However, if one looks beyond his façade of irascibleness and recalcitrance, one will find a very compassionate, progressive, and humourous man who genuinely cared for people and merely wanted to subvert the iniquities afflicting our world.

While revelations of Tosh's deep spirituality and wicked sense of humour came as no surprise, I cannot tell a lie, when I first heard about his love of children, especially infants, my jaw dropped. I had a hard time envisioning him cradling a baby, let alone cooing to one. Additionally, I found knowledge about his culinary skills stunning. With his macho image, somehow, the concept of him delighting in this domesticity was hard to harmonise. Of all the insightful lessons I learned from the contributors to this work, the most eyebrow-raising however, was Tosh's desire to fly and his belief in his ability to do so. Up until now, I was unfamiliar with this concept of humans' potential to fly and would say that premise defies logic. Now that I know research has been conducted on this theory, it reinforces for me Tosh's open-mindedness and expansiveness.

While my admiration for Mr Tosh was initially spawned from my appreciation of his music and basic knowledge of his principles, being privy to more intimate details about him from those who knew him well has resulted in my holding him in even higher esteem. He was indeed a remarkable man! One who should be celebrated instead of denigrated. I hope that in my lifetime, the prevailing dismissive attitude towards him will eventually dissipate, or at least, be tempered with empathy for his foibles.

Ceil Tulloch

Contributors' Biographies

Jayne Cortez

The multi-award winning Jayne Cortez was one of America's most avant-garde poets. In 1964 she established the Watts Repertory Theater in Watts, California, and served as the artistic director from 1964 to 1970. Later, she created Bola Press, and has written and published more than ten books of poetry. Her works have been translated into 28 different languages, and she has been published in well-known journals such as *Présence Africaine*, *Black Scholar, Daughters of Africa* and *Mother Jones*. A staunch advocate of civil and political rights she was also the organiser of the international symposium 'Slave Routes: Resistance, Abolition & Creative Progress' (NYU) and director of the film, *Yari Yari Pamberi: Black Women Writers Dissecting Globalization*. She was co-founder and president of the Organization of Women Writers of Africa, Inc., has participated in the Round Table: 'Dialogue Among Civilizations,' at the United Nations Millennium Summit 2000, and can be seen on screen in the films *Women In Jazz* and *Poetry In Motion*.

Dr Omar Davies

Dr Omar Davies is the Minister of Transport, Works and Housing in the Government of Jamaica, and a Member of Parliament for the South St Andrew constituency, which includes the community of Trench Town. Trench Town spawned many of the artists who became icons in the development of Jamaica's pop music, including Bob Marley, Peter Tosh, Alton Ellis and Delroy Wilson.

Lowell 'Sly' Dunbar

Born in the Waterhouse district of East Kingston, Jamaica, 'Sly' is one half of the dynamic 'Riddim Twins.' Affectionately called Sly 'Drumbar,' he is Jamaica's premier drummer, and has had the privilege of collaborating with many of the world's most influential musicians in reggae, R&B, blues, soul, and rock. Along with his close friend and music partner Robbie Shakespeare, Sly has produced and released more than 200,000 tracks and 45 albums. In 2010, the duo received a double Grammy award nomination for *Made in Jamaica*, and *One Pop Reggae*. Previously, they won a Grammy for their 1998 album, *Friends*, and another in 1984, for *Anthem*, while a part of Black Uhuru. Mr Dunbar is also the producer at his and Robbie Shakespeare's Taxi Records label.

George 'Fully' Fullwood

George 'Fully' Fullwood is a titan of Jamaican music. A native of Kingston, he started his musical odyssey as a guitarist, while a boy attending Greenwich Farm basic school, before adopting the bass. With several friends, he formed the band Riddim Raiders in the 1960s, and performed rocksteady and ska mento music at the Labour Right and Boys Clubs in his neighbourhood. The founder of the 1970s Jamaican reggae band Soul Syndicate, Fullwood has played a vital role in the development and popularity of Jamaican music for more than four decades. He has collaborated on hundreds of projects with every major Jamaican reggae artist, including the late Bob Marley, Peter Tosh, Dennis Brown, and Gregory Isaacs to name a few, enriching their music with his bass sounds.

Revd Canon Ernle Gordon

Canon Ernle Gordon, was the rector of St Mary the Virgin Anglican Church for over 35 years, and had been a pastor for more than 45 years. In addition to ministering to his congregation, he has written articles for the Jamaican newspapers, and has done radio broadcasts and lectures on theological theory. In 2010, Canon Gordon received special acknowledgement for his ministry, from the Bishop of Jamaica and The Cayman Islands, the Right Reverend Alfred Reid, during the special '50 Years of Ministry' to the communities celebration. Previously, he had served as a member of the Jamaica National Heritage Trust (JNHT) Board from 2006 to 2009, and also as a former Vice President of the Jamaica Council of Churches.

Dermot Hussey

Dermot Hussey is one of Jamaica's most venerated media personalities and musicologists. He has more than three decades of experience as a journalist, film director, broadcaster and radio host. Some of the highlights of his illustrious career include interviews with Bob Marley, Quincy Jones, and Harry Belafonte, and the production of the 1987 documentary *Peter Tosh Remembered*. Additionally, he is the co-author of *Bob Marley: Reggae King of the World*. In the 1980s, the Jamaica government officially recognised Mr Hussey for his sterling service to Music and Media by awarding him a Musgrave Medal. A staunch believer in the preservation of Jamaica's rich music/cultural heritage, Mr Hussey donated his entire collection of vinyl record albums, tapes (reel-to-reel, cassette), films, and documents to the Jamaica Music Museum in 2010.

Donald Kinsey

Born in Gary, Indiana to the late legendary bluesman Lester 'Big Daddy' Kinsey, Donald followed in his father's musical footsteps while ensuring his own imprint on music as a professional blues and reggae guitarist. A master of his craft, Kinsey has lent his musical talents to the likes of the late blues notable Albert King, and reggae stellars Peter Tosh and Bob Marley. He has also collaborated with the Rolling Stones, the Staple Singers, and the Chosen Ones. In 1984, at the end of

Tosh's 'Mama Africa' tour Kinsey turned his attention to creating blues music with his family members. As such, he banded with his siblings to form their new band, the Kinsey Report, and simultaneously recorded with them and his father on several albums.

Chuck Krall

Chuck Krall is an independent, professional photojournalist based in Los Angeles, California. He has worked extensively in the music and entertainment industries, photographing subjects in the genres of country, rock, reggae, jazz, pop, and R&B. While a Peace Corps volunteer in Jamaica, he got his first break taking photos for the organisation. Five years later, he became the late reggae artist, Bob Marley's tour photographer. His work has also been utilised by major record companies such as Columbia, Epic, Warner Brothers, Capitol, Polydor, Arista and Motown, and also by various radio stations. Additionally, he has done assignments for national publications including *Time*, *Newsweek*, *People*, *US*, and the *National Enquirer*. Trade publications like *Billboard*, *Record World, Cash Box*, and *Radio & Records* have also benefitted from his talent.

Herbie Miller

Herbie Miller is a leading authority on Jamaican music. After managing Peter Tosh, he went on to manage many other outstanding Jamaican talents such as Big Youth, the Skatalites, and Toots and the Maytals to name a few. In addition to managing artists/bands, Miller also wrote liner notes for the Skatalites, Bob Marley, and several Peter Tosh albums. During his 30 plus years of involvement with the music industry, he both recorded and staged concerts for musicians of ska, reggae, and jazz both locally and internationally. He later worked in the capacity of A&R for Profile Records in the USA, and also as a consultant, lending his expertise to major record labels that include Island Records, Sony, and Def Jam. Mr Miller was also instrumental in opening up the Japanese music market over a seven-year period, by co-ordinating and staging huge annual reggae tours to Japan with the production called, 'Reggae Japan Splash.' Today, he is the Director/Curator of the Jamaica Music Museum and also a revered ethnomusicologist with a specialisation in Caribbean identity and slave culture.

Norman 'Otis' Richmond

Norman O. Richmond, aka Jalali, is a Toronto-based radio personality, journalist, and activist. Furthermore, he is a cofounder of the Black Music Association/Toronto Chapter (BMA/TC), and has recorded several reggae singles in Toronto. A man with a social conscience and a profound sense of responsibility to the black community, Mr Richmond lends his support to numerous organisations. Additionally, he contributes articles to the Uhurunews.com and Pan-African News blogs. He is a recipient of the 1992 Toronto Arts Award and also a 'Toast & Roast' in 2009, for his significant contribution and commitment to the arts and culture in Toronto.

Desmond Shakespeare

Fondly called 'Shakes' by his peers, Desmond Shakespeare is the quintessential businessman. After working as a Senior Industrial Engineer at the CARICOM Secretariat and as a Consultant at Jamaica Trade & Invest (JAMPRO) for almost a decade, Shakes decided to broaden his horizon and became Managing Partner at Quorum Business Management located in Kingston, Jamaica, where his background and expertise in music/entertainment and small business development can be optimally utilised. Shakespeare is also a musicologist, who has researched the early development of contemporary Jamaican popular music and has worked with Peter Tosh, Sly Dunbar, and Robbie Shakespeare among others.

Robbie Shakespeare

Also known as Robbie 'Basspeare' Shakespeare is the other half of the prolific 'Riddim Twins.' While attending Vauxhall Secondary School in Jamaica, he took piano lessons. He later honed his piano playing skills as an adult when he began performing professionally. He also became proficient in playing the rhythm section of the guitar and was adept at creating numerous rhythm styles. The bass became his instrument of choice after he was exposed to the playing of the bassist, Ashton 'Family Man' Barrett of Bob Marley and the Wailers. In synergy with his close friend and associate for nearly four decades, 'Sly' Dunbar, he has created and produced reggae rhythms that flavour the music of the who's who from diverse music genres and continues to enchant music lovers with his eclectic and innovative sounds.

Roger Steffens

Roger 'Ras Rojah' Steffens began his media career on the radio in 1961 and was one of the pioneer disc jockeys instrumental in introducing reggae music to audiences in the US. After honing his skills in New York, he expanded his horizons by relocating to Los Angeles where he gained employment at KCRW radio station. His vast knowledge of reggae and enthusiasm for the subject matter resulted in him co-hosting with Hank Holmes, the station's popular Sunday reggae programme, 'The Reggae Beat,' which ran from 1979 to 1994, and of which Bob Marley was the first guest. The phenomenal success of this award-winning show led the enterprising Steffens to start his own reggae TV show and also cofound the *Beat* magazine in May 1982. After a stint at Island Records, Steffens accepted and has continued to hold the position of chairman of the Reggae Grammy Committee since its inception in 1985. Additionally, he has lectured extensively on Bob Marley and Peter Tosh both in the US and overseas, and has made invaluable contributions to music documentaries such as VH1's *Behind the Music* series on Bob Marley and Peter Tosh.

Dennis Thompson

Dennis Thompson is both a studio and live engineer par excellence. Thompson made his foray into music as a sound system operator at the Lotus-a-Go-Go club in Half Way Tree, Kingston. Upon leaving the Lotus, he worked at venerated establishments such as Randy's Studio, the Merritone Music (which produced the Merritone Sound System), and New Dimension Studios. After migrating to New York City in 1973, he continued to hone his craft and blaze a trail as a professional engineer for many of the household names in the world of music. In February 2011, the Jamaica Reggae Industry Association (JaRIA) honoured him with an award for his outstanding contribution to music as a studio engineer.

Doug Wendt

A jack of all trades, Doug Wendt is a celebrated filmmaker, music consultant, DJ/VJ, writer, band leader, performer, producer and also an adjunct professor of Film History at Montana State University since 2007. He has been making his mark in the Entertainment industry since the mid-1960s. Wendt was the first American DJ to host a commercial radio show dedicated to reggae music. A reggae aficionado, he fell in love with reggae in 1973, after watching Jimmy Cliff in the movie *The Harder They Come*, and seeing The Wailers live in concert at the Matrix in San Francisco.

Dick Wingate

Dick Wingate has worn numerous hats in key leadership positions in companies such as Columbia Records (Director of Product Management), CBS Records/Epic Records (Director of Talent Acquisition), PolyGram Records (Senior Vice-President, A & R), InTouch Group (Vice-President of Market

Development), Arista Records/BMG (Senior Vice-President, Marketing), BMG Entertainment (New Media Consultant), online music and software company Liquid Audio (Senior Vice-President of Content Development and Label Relations) and is a member of the National Academy of Recording Arts and Sciences.

At the Roxy Theatre in Los Angeles, California, 1983 during a sound check for his last show in LA
©Roger Steffens/Roger Steffens's Reggae Archives

Lightning Source UK Ltd.
Milton Keynes UK
UKOW06f1515210415

250038UK00011B/72/P